Four
Temperaments

Astrology &

Personality
Testing

Bethel Baptist Church
P.O. BOX 167
AUMSVILLE, OR 97325

Four Temperaments

Astrology &

Personality Testing

Martin and Deidre Bobgan

EastGate Publishers
Santa Barbara, CA 93110

Scripture quotations in this book are from the King James
Version, unless otherwise stated.

**FOUR TEMPERAMENTS, ASTROLOGY
& PERSONALITY TESTING**

Copyright © 1992 Martin and Deidre Bobgan
Published by EastGate Publishers
4137 Primavera Road
Santa Barbara, CA 93110

Library of Congress Catalog Card Number 92-81219
ISBN 0-941717-07-0

Printed in the United States of America.

In this book we name people in reference to what they have taught or written. While we are critical of their promotion and use of psychological theories and techniques, we are not questioning their sincerity or their faith. When we discuss their teachings, we are dealing with issues, not personalities.

Martin and Deidre Bobgan

TABLE OF CONTENTS

1

Christians
and the
Four Temperaments

Numerous Christians believe they can gain great insight into themselves and others by studying the personality characteristics of the four temperaments. Authors claim to tell you "why you act the way you do" and how to:

- "Analyze your strengths and weaknesses."
- "Discover how God can use your gifts."
- "Improve your relationships with others."
- "Get ahead in your career."[1]

Testimonies abound. After years of marriage, a woman reads a book about the four temperaments and believes she understands her husband for the first time. Mothers are convinced that once they

discover whether their children are little San-
guines, Cholerics, Melancholies, or Phlegmatics,
then they will be able to understand why their children behave the way they do.

Many temperament enthusiasts believe that
knowing the temperaments gives them greater
ability in relating to their friends. They claim to
know which type will be late for lunch, which will
be prompt, and which will be early. And once they
begin to use the four temperaments system, they
are convinced it is accurate and reliable.

What Are the Four Temperaments?

The four temperaments theory is an ancient
system devised for understanding human nature
and thereby improving the human condition. The
theory divides people according to various personality characteristics that appear to make up their
basic temperament. Some people attempt to distinguish between a person's temperament and his personality by saying that temperament traits are
inborn while personality traits are the result of
nature and nurture. However, the distinction is not
always possible or clear.

The four temperament categories are Sanguine,
Choleric, Melancholy, and Phlegmatic. Each category or type is defined by a list of descriptive terms.
Then people are assigned to one or more types by
matching the person with the descriptions.

The following chart presents each of the four
temperaments with a brief list of traits generally
associated with each temperament.

Sanguine	Choleric	Melancholy	Phlegmatic
Cheerful	Optimistic	Melancholy	Calm
Friendly	Active	Sensitive	Dependable
Talkative	Confident	Analytical	Efficient
Lively	Strong-willed	Perfectionistic	Easy-going
Restless	Quick to anger	Unsociable	Passive
Self-centered	Aggressive	Moody	Stubborn
Undependable	Inconsiderate	Rigid	Lazy

The above list is both brief and incomplete. As the theory has been passed down through the centuries, the descriptions of each type have been modified and expanded. Descriptive terms for each type are not always consistent among those who use the four temperaments system. For some, a particular characteristic, such as *leadership*, would be used to describe the Choleric; for others it would describe the Sanguine. Thus, the lists are not hard and fast. They vary according to the person who is presenting them.

General or Specific?

Temperament categories are very broad and general. They are not specific. Yet, when various writers describe the temperaments, the descriptions can sound very specific and exact. Notice, for example, how specific the following description of the Sanguine personality sounds. It was written by the 18th century philosopher Immanuel Kant.

. . . the sanguine person is carefree and full of hope; attributes great importance to whatever he may be dealing with at the moment, but may have forgotten all about it the next. He means to keep his promises but fails to do so because he never considered deeply enough beforehand whether he would be able to keep them. He is good-natured enough to help others but is a bad debtor and constantly asks for time to pay. He is very sociable, given to pranks, contented, does not take anything very seriously, and has many, many friends. He is not vicious but difficult to convert from his sins; he may repent but this contrition (which never becomes a feeling of guilt) is soon forgotten. He is easily fatigued and bored by work but is constantly engaged in mere games—these carry with them constant change, and persistence is not his forte.[2]

Creativity is always involved in describing a typical Sanguine, Choleric, Melancholy, or Phlegmatic. Such temperament descriptions generally resemble characters in movies or books more than any kind of scientifically established categories by which to analyze people.

Why Are the Four Temperaments Popular?

The four temperaments, which had largely gone out of vogue since medieval times, have become popular among evangelical Christians in the same way that astrology has risen in popularity among nonChristians. Perhaps because of life's ever-increasing complexities and numerous complex psychological systems, people are looking for simple ways to understand themselves and others.

And that's why the four temperaments have made a comeback. They are easy to understand and use. They offer simple explanations for the complexity of individual differences and propose simple solutions to complex problems of living. Furthermore, many Christians have confidence in the four temperaments theory because they believe it is reliable, helpful, and compatible with the Bible.

From the beginning, typologies have been designed to help people both understand themselves and improve their condition. Each of the four temperaments has positive and negative characteristics. Positive traits are called "strengths" and negative ones are called "weaknesses." Thus, the idea is to help people understand themselves and others through identifying positive and negative traits.

Then once they understand themselves according to their strengths and weaknesses, they can work to enhance their strengths and overcome their weaknesses. Furthermore, once they have put each other into boxes they won't be as surprised when negative traits surface in behavior. There will be an illusion of being able to predict behavior.

True and Reliable?

The four temperaments theory also gives an illusion of truth. One can apply all descriptive traits to all humans to a greater or lesser degree.

Therefore, when temperament characteristics are placed in categories, people can easily see themselves because of the universal nature of traits, such as friendly, confident, sensitive, dependable, and so on.

Then, when people are told that they may be a combination of the four temperaments, they can easily fit themselves into a classification. That does not mean the four temperaments are in themselves accurate or helpful. It only means they consist of universal traits and that people can identify with them to some degree.

The four temperaments are broad, arbitrarily defined categories of universally applicable descriptive words that apply to large numbers of people. Yet, when people apply categories to themselves and others, they think they have specific information. Actually they may have some broad approximation which might be partly true in a very general sense. This is referred to in research literature as the Barnum Effect, named after the circus showman P. T. Barnum.

In their book *Astrology: Do the Heavens Rule Our Destiny?* John Ankerberg and John Weldon declare that the "chart of any person is potentially relevant to every other person,"[3] Just as in astrology, a particular four temperaments category is potentially relevant to everyone. As we will show later, there are more variation possibilities among the twelve zodiac signs than with the four temperaments. Thus, their statement would be even more applicable to the four temperaments.

In spite of the lack of scientific evidence or biblical scholarship, books about identifying and transforming temperaments often sound authoritative. They include both plausible information and wild speculation presented as proven fact. Once a person is hooked into such a system of understanding self and others, he will see everything from that perspective. Also, once a person is convinced that he fits a particular category or combination of categories, he will look for and notice confirming evidence. He will look for validation and find it even when it is not there. He will even tend to act according to his new understanding. In other words he will make himself fit that category.

Peter Glick, in his article "Stars In Our Eyes," says the tendency to look for and notice confirming evidence explains why, "despite the lack of any evidence of their validity . . . millions of people turn daily to horoscopes for clues to leading their lives."[4] The same is true of the four temperaments. They appear to be true because people want them to be true. They appear to work because people want them to work.

Greater Understanding?

Another reason for their popularity is that knowledge of the four temperaments may also give the illusion of exceptional insight into oneself and others. By using lists of descriptive words and phrases, people assign themselves and others to Sanguine, Choleric, Melancholy, and Phlegmatic categories. The assumption is that once they have placed someone in a category, they can understand and know that person better. However, the whole process of putting a person into a category leads to no substantial additional understanding of anyone.

The process of categorizing self and others relies on previous subjective knowledge. All that happens is that the subjective knowledge one already has about a person is organized according to an artificial arrangement and given a name. For instance, if you "discover" that your child is "Phlegmatic," you were already familiar with enough of his characteristics to line them up with the adjectives listed under "Phlegmatic."

All you have done is to match descriptive characteristics and come up with a name: "Phlegmatic." But, since the list could not have included everything about your child, the word *Phlegmatic* may be inaccurate and misleading. You might actually understand your child less for having matched the available adjectives, because you might now focus on those characteristics and ignore others that might be far more important.

Knowing the temperament traits and categories can actually hinder knowing and understanding ourselves and others. For instance, one characteristic may be noticed in a person in a particular situation. Then, as quick as a flash, that person is popped into a category and assigned the other characteristics associated with that temperament, whether or not the other characteristics specifically apply. As soon as a person is placed into a temperament category, there is a tendency to view that person accordingly. Then the temperament user may simply react to the label, rather than respond to him as a real, living person.

Using temperament or personality typologies undermines the complex variety of individual differences expressed within the vast possibility of social interactions and circumstances. People are not exactly the same in different circumstances. One who may appear reserved and quiet in some circumstances may be highly expressive and outgoing in others.

An Excuse for Behavior?

Another reason for the four temperaments' popularity may be their fleshly appeal. Those who encourage Christians to utilize the four temperaments for spiritual growth consistently warn against using temperament weaknesses as excuses for behavior. Unfortunately, that is a great temptation—to move from "understanding" why I act a certain way to "excusing" sinful behavior because of "my temperament." Whenever sinful behavior is relabeled "weaknesses," there is a dwindling sense of responsibility and a gnawing sense of being trapped in helplessness. Once resigned to one's weakness, one may attempt to "make up" for that "weakness" by developing and focusing on the so-called "strengths" of the particular temperament one thinks he has.

An Appeal to the Flesh and Pride?

While some may be tempted to use their temperament type to excuse behavior, others may be attracted to positive qualities associated with their particular type. Every category has positive characteristics that a person may apply to himself.

It is easy for many people to fit themselves into several categories through lists of positive characteristics. It is when negative characteristics come along that people tend to shy away from certain categories and limit themselves mainly to one category—as long as the positive outweighs the negative. The four temperaments seem to work because of positive illusions people have about themselves.

The further temptation then is to become proud of one's own temperament and one's own self. "Oh, yes, I'm a Sanguine. I'm outgoing, friendly, warm, and enthusiastic. However, I'm not inconsistent, so I must be partly Phlegmatic." Indeed, one can pick and choose among the characteristics and come up with a very enticing, deceptive conception of self simply by applying attractive characteristics to oneself.

Whenever there is a system which encourages people to analyze themselves, the self-focus can lead to pride. Or, it can lead to reverse pride—self-pity or any of the other self-preoccupying activities of mind and heart.

Better Communication?

Other reasons for the four temperaments' popularity are the direct and implied promises for improving communication. When temperament book authors suggest ways to improve communication through understanding the four temperaments, there is an underlying requirement to figure out the temperament of one's spouse, children, business associates, and others with whom one might desire better communication. All kinds of people who profess Christianity are analyzing themselves and others according to the four temperaments. Rather than communicating on the basis of love and truth as revealed in Scripture, they are attempting to manipulate the relationships to fit temperament strengths and weaknesses. Indeed, using the temperaments can turn spontaneous interactions into manipulative interchanges.

Self-Improvement or Sanctification?

Best-selling books on the four temperaments and other similar typologies give people the idea they can change themselves for good as long as they have this special knowledge. Some people think that through this particular knowledge they can replace their weaknesses with their strengths and thereby enhance their own identity and improve their behavior. Promises of improvement and change abound in books that offer "transformed temperaments."

Some books equate the sinful human nature with the four temperaments and the fruit of the Spirit with the so-called new temperament a Christian gets when he is born again. The books offer even more than self-improvement; they offer a brand new temperament to bring out and enhance the strengths of the existing temperament, which has already been identified as the sinful nature.

Thus, through the religion of the four temperaments, new birth supposedly gives one a new temperament, which supposedly improves and enhances the old, sinful, natural temperament. Obviously attempting to wed the four temperaments theory with the doctrines of salvation and sanctification leads to a great deal of theological confusion.

Rather than clarifying the biblical doctrines of man—creation, salvation, and sanctification—focusing on the four temperaments muddies the water. Worse yet, the four temperaments theology poisons the pure water of The Word.

When one uses the Bible to promote pet theories and transmogrifies the fruit of the Spirit into temperament traits, one ends up with a religion of works. At best, studying the four temperaments may aid in very superficial self-improvement. But, even that possibility has not been scientifically verified. The crux of the matter is this: should Christians learn and utilize the four temperaments theory of personality or any other psychological theory of personality for purposes of understanding human nature and progressing in their spiritual life?

Compatible with Scripture?

Many Christians are captivated by the popularized four temperaments doctrines, because they have been convinced that the teachings are compatible with Scripture. We are living in a psychologized society. Many Christians have become counseling psychologists who attempt to integrate their pet psychological theories and therapies with Christianity. Each psychologist or counselor who tries to integrate psychological theories with Christianity believes that his combination is biblical. He may be incorporating personality theories of Sigmund Freud, Carl Jung, Alfred Adler, Abraham Maslow, Fritz Perls, Carl Rogers, Albert Ellis, and/or Viktor Frankl. However, there are serious problems with attempts to integrate psychological theories of personality with the Bible.

The primary problem is that such personality and counseling theories offer unbiblical explanations about who man is, how he should live, and how to change him. While there may seem to be points of agreement, such as the importance of love, at base such theories are antithetical to Christianity. Each presents a world view devoid of God. Each gives an unbiblical philosophy of life (who man is, why he is here, and how he should live). And, each offers another means of salvation and sanctification. Therefore psychological theories of personality are actually rival religious systems.

The four temperaments and other personality type systems did not originate from Scripture. They are part of that philosophical/psychological pool of man-made systems and personal opinions which attempt to explain the nature of man and present methods for change. Christian authors promoting the four temperaments and similar typologies base their ideas on unproven psychological theories and subjective observations which are based on neither the rigors of scientific investigation nor the rigors of exegetical Bible study.

Personality theories and temperament typologies are filled with human notions about the nature of man, how he is to live, and how he changes. Temperament tests and personality inventories also are based upon the same flimsy foundation of psychological subjectivity rather than on science or the Bible.

What Kind of Psychology?

As in our other books, when we speak of psychological theories, therapies, and techniques, we are **not** referring to the entire discipline of psychology. Our concern is with that part of psychology which deals with the very nature of man, how he should live, and how he changes. Because such theories deal with the nonphysical aspects of the person, they intrude upon the very essence of biblical doctrines of man, including his fallen condition, salvation, sanctification, and relationship of love and obedience to God. Psychological theories offer a variety of alternative explanations about the human condition, but they are merely scientific-sounding opinions and speculations.

Throughout this book we refer to research studies, because if a case can be made for the use of any kind of psychology, it must be supported in the research. We want to make it perfectly clear, however, that we believe the Bible stands on its own. It does not need scientific verification or support. Christian presuppositions begin with Scripture, and any information culled from the environment is answerable to Scripture, not vice versa.

Therefore, we do not use research results to prove the Bible is right. That is totally unnecessary. We cite research to reveal the unscientific nature of the kinds of psychological theories and techniques that seem to be popular among evangelical Christians.

As we continue here to address our concerns about the prevalent promotion of psychological opinions, we will look at the history and development of the four temperaments and how they relate to the practice of astrology. We will also examine other personality typologies, personality inventories and profiles, and the basic assumptions underlying their use, in terms of whether they are scientifically valid, practically useful, or biblically sound. And finally, we will consider a biblical alternative to personality typologies and tests.

2

Occult Origins of the Four Temperaments

A brief look at the history of the four temperaments will reveal that their origins lie in ancient myths and occult practices. From ancient times through the Middle Ages, physicians and philosophers used their understanding of the four humors (bodily fluids), the four temperaments, and signs of the zodiac to treat diseases and understand individual differences among people.

Greek cosmology's four elements are basic to the four temperament personality theory. Greek philosopher Empedocles (495-425 B.C.) taught that there were four primary elements in the known universe: fire, air, earth and water. Each had specific qualities of warm, cold, dry, and moist with fire being warm and dry; air being warm and moist; earth being cold and dry; and water being cold and moist.[1] Because of the inherent mixture of cosmology with mythology, each element also had its corresponding god or goddess. In writing about the four elements, Empedocles said:

> First, therefore, let me tell you of all that there is the four roots: Zeus the resplendent, the life-bearing Hera, and Aïdoneus, and Nestis who in her tears is spilling man's fountain of life.[2]

Zeus is the fire, Hera the air, Aïdoneus the earth, and Nestis the water. The four elements and their qualities were also part of early Greek astrology.[3]

Hippocrates (460-377 B.C.) later expanded on Empedocles' theory of four elements and taught that there were four corresponding bodily fluids or humors: blood, yellow bile, black bile, and phlegm. He theorized that health depended upon the proper balance of those humors in the body and that illnesses were caused by an imbalance of the bodily fluids.[4] Hippocrates also taught that there was a relationship between the bodily fluids and the yearly seasons with seasonal variations of each fluid. For instance, phlegm was noted to increase in the winter and be the weakest in summer.[5] (An early theory of the common cold?)

Hippocrates believed that people had different proportions of the humors with one humor more or less dominant. Thus his scheme of relationships among the elements and their qualities, the bodily fluids (humor), and the seasons would look like this:

Element	Qualities	Humor	Type	Season
Air	Warm/Moist	Blood	Sanguine	Spring
Fire	Warm/Dry	Yellow Bile	Choleric	Summer
Earth	Cold/Dry	Black Bile	Melancholy	Autumn
Water	Cold/Moist	Phlegm	Phlegmatic	Winter

Hippocrates is generally credited with the humoral temperament theory of personality, since he connected the types with both mental and physical states. For instance, blood, being warm and moist, made the cheeks rosy and promoted a cheerful (Sanguine) temperament. Phlegm, on the other hand, was considered cold and moist and brought about watery-looking, colorless skin and a bland or sluggish temperament. However, Hippocrates gave his primary attention to the humors as they related to disease rather than to personality. And while he developed the original idea of bodily fluids corresponding to the four elements and saw connections between bodily fluids and temperament, he did not fully develop the temperament theory of personality types.

Others continued to use and build on Hippocrates' original premises. For instance, Plato (427-347 B.C.), who had studied under Socrates, contended that madness resulted from morbid humors contacting a person's mortal soul.[6] Plato taught that the qualities of the elements and the constitution of the humors related directly to behavior. He said:

> The truth is that the intemperance of love is a disease of the soul due chiefly to the

> moisture and fluidity which is produced in one of the elements by the loose consistency of the bones.[7]

Plato continued his erroneous dialogue by arguing that bad behavior was at least partly caused by the bodily condition:

> For no man is voluntarily bad; but the bad become bad by reason of an ill disposition of the body and bad education, things which are hateful to every man and happen to him against his will.[8]

Plato then explained how that happened:

> For where the acid and briny phlegm and other bitter and bilious humours wander about in the body, and find no exit or escape, but are pent up within and mingle their own vapours with the motions of the soul, and are blended . . . and being carried to the three places of the soul . . . they create infinite varieties of ill-temper and melancholy, of rashness and cowardice, and also of forgetfulness and stupidity.[9]

Plato's student Aristotle (384-322 B.C.) believed that the shape of the body reflected the activities of the soul as well. He was interested in how the humors were involved in forming the body and the mind. He associated warm, thick blood with strength and cold, thin blood with intelligence.[10]

Aristotle also wrote extensively about the relationship of black bile to a melancholy temperament.[11] Because he strongly believed Hippocrates' humoral theory, Aristotle concluded that mental and emotional disturbances were of physical origin.[12]

Claudius Galen of Pergamum (A.D. 130-200) was the physician who advanced Hippocrates' theories and took them to the Roman world. He built on Hippocrates' original theories and wrote more fully on the relationship between humors and temperaments. He sought to explain emotional and behavioral differences between people and to develop treatments that would be suitable to those of varying temperaments.[13] In fact, some of his descriptions of physiological characteristics and their relationship to personality were quite detailed. Everything could presumably be explained by a balance of the humors with the qualities of warm, cold, dry, and moist. For instance Galen wrote:

> Those who are warmer are more hairy and irascible . . . . If their thighs show dense hair they are very lecherous. . . . But if somebody has much hair on the chest, his body is not necessarily much hotter, since most of his heat is in his heart and therefore he is more passionate. . . . But if his skin is hairless, smooth and white, then he becomes cowardly, timid and unenterprising.[14]

Galen combined elemental qualities and bodily humors with more specific personality characteristics. Briefly his scheme would look like this:

Element	Qualities	Humor	Type	Traits
Air	Warm/Moist	Blood	Sanguine	cheerful warm
Fire	Warm/Dry	Yellow Bile	Choleric	quick to anger
Earth	Cold/Dry	Black Bile	Melancholy	melan-choly
Water	Cold/Moist	Phlegm	Phlegmatic	placid, sluggish

The word *temperament* itself comes from the Latin word *temperamentum* which meant "proper mixing." The idea was that if the bodily fluids were tempered, that is, reduced in their intensity by balancing the humors with each other, then healing would occur. Because the early Greeks and Romans believed that the bodily fluids were influenced by the universal presence of the four elements (air, fire, earth and water), they also believed that balance could be altered by atmospheric changes. Even the positions of various planets were thought to alter the fluids for better or worse because it was believed there was a "direct relationship between the macrocosm of the universe and the microcosm of the organism." They further believed that "contraries should be cured by contraries."[15] This is very similar to the astrological concept of polarities and the present-day attempts to balance negative personality characteristics with their opposites.

Early Link with Astrology.

The four temperaments theory of personality was intrinsically tied to another corresponding system of typing personality: the astrological signs of the zodiac. The *Encyclopedia of Psychology* says:

> Though the shifting patterns in the sky were first studied for the sake of finding portents of events that would affect the life of the group, a rationale for the relationship between personal traits and time of birth began to evolve well before the beginning of the Christian era. Central to astrological views of personality is a system of 12 patterns or types that correspond to the 12 signs of the zodiac. The 12 types may be viewed as including three modes of expression of each of the four elements noted by Empedocles, as there are said to be three air signs, three earth signs, three fire signs, and three water signs. This typology has enjoyed some popularity for over 2000 years.[16]

The twelve zodiac personality types are arranged in four sets with three signs in each set. These are called *trigons* or *triplicities*. Each triplicity corresponds with one of the four elements of Empedocles. Furthermore, each triplicity corresponds with one of Hippocrates' four humors. And each triplicity corresponds with one of the four temperaments. From Empedocles to Galen, each person who developed those categories also believed in the influences of the planets and stars on the elements, humors and temperaments.

The connection between personalities based upon bodily fluids and personalities based upon the arrangements of heavenly bodies was the astrological belief that each person is a microcosm of the macrocosm (the universe). Another ancient astrological saying was "as above, so below." The following chart reveals the link between the four temperaments and the zodiac signs:

Element	Humor	Temperament	Zodiac
Air	Blood	Sanguine	Gemini
			Libra
			Aquarius
Fire	Yellow Bile	Choleric	Aries
			Leo
			Sagittarius
Earth	Black Bile	Melancholy	Taurus
			Virgo
			Capricorn
Water	Phlegm	Phlegmatic	Cancer
			Scorpio
			Pisces

The connection between the four temperaments and the zodiac is not coincidental. Although much of what Galen wrote did not include astrology, two of his works focused on astrological medicine. In his *Prognostication of Disease by Astrology*, Galen presented his theory of how the relative arrangement of the moon, the signs of the zodiac, and the planets could guide a physician in treating disease.

Through these astrological configurations, relative to an individual's dominant humor and temperament, Galen believed that he could foretell what diseases a person would have, what treatment should be given, and what the prognosis would be.[17]

In his book *Psychological Types*, Carl Jung also clearly notes the relationship between astrology and the four temperaments. He says:

> From the earliest times attempts have been made to classify individuals according to types, and so to bring order into the chaos. The oldest attempts known to us were made by oriental astrologers who devised the so-called trigons of the four elements—air, water, earth, and fire. The air trigon in the horoscope consists of the three aerial signs of the zodiac, Aquarius, Gemini, Libra; the fire trigon is made up of Aries, Leo, Sagittarius. According to this age-old view, whoever is born in these trigons shares in their aerial or fiery nature and will have a corresponding temperament and fate. Closely connected with this ancient cosmological scheme is the physiological typology of antiquity, the division into four temperaments corresponding to the four humours. What was first represented by the signs of the zodiac was later expressed in the physiological language of Greek medicine, giving us the classification into the phlegmatic, sanguine, choleric, and melancholic. These are simply designations

for the secretions of the body. As is well known, this typology lasted at least seventeen hundred years. As for the astrological type theory, to the astonishment of the enlightened it still remains intact today, and is even enjoying a new vogue.[18]

The Middle Ages.

Galen's four temperaments personality theory continued to be used well into medieval times within its original context of astrology. In his article for the *Encyclopedia of Psychology*, K. J. Shapiro says:

> Synthesizing ideas from classical Greek medicine and astronomy, a theory of temperaments prevailing well into medieval times held that, for example, a sanguine disposition reflected a particular combination of humors in the body and that, in turn, this combination had been fixed by a certain configuration of the stars at the time of an individual's birth.[19]

People commonly believed that they had acquired their temperament from being born under a certain astrological sign and that their bodily fluids were subject to planetary influences. Thus, many physicians during the Middle Ages were also astrologers.

The medieval view of man, nature, and the universe reflected Greek ideas having to do with the four elements, the four humors, the four temperaments, and astrology. In his book *The Mind of the Middle Ages*, Frederick Artz says:

> The structure of man, the microcosm, followed the structure of the universe, the macrocosm. . . .There was built up out of Greek science, religious ideas, and folklore an immense and intertwined tangle of astrology, alchemy, chemistry, geography, and other sciences.[20]

The close connection between astrology and the four temperaments can also be seen in this description of medieval alchemy:

> The medieval alchemist believed, following the tradition of the great Aristotle, that man's body, like all other material things, was composed of four elements, earth, air, fire and water. Each individual had his own particular mixture of these—his *temperamentum*, as they called it. This was determined at conception and birth by the influence of the constellations and planets. The aptitudes, weaknesses and chances of success or failure of each human being sprang from his elemental composition. Since no one had been properly mixed since Adam, the problem emerged of discovering some sovereign remedy—*secretum maximum*—which would cleanse and rectify man's composition and so produce a superman, full of physical and mental vigor and

enjoying a life prolonged through many joyous centuries. Hence the persistent search for the Elixir, or philosopher's stone, which should produce these marvelous results, as well as transform the baser metals into gold.[21]

In spite of being condemned by churchmen during the Middle Ages, many clerics followed astrological principles when practicing medicine. In her book *Suggestion of the Devil*, Dr. Judith Neaman declares that medieval charts, diagrams and aphoristic poems prove that astrology was used together with the four humors and temperaments both in medicine and in daily affairs. The medieval view of personality was that the arrangement of stars and planets in the zodiac determined each person's personality both at birth and throughout his life.

Later typologies.

Through the years, philosophers, psychiatrists, and psychologists have devised numerous typologies to classify people according to social behavior, modes of feeling and perceiving, attitudes, and even bodily physique as it might relate to temperament.

The four temperaments were finally devalued and considered relics of limited, ancient attempts to understand and deal with individual differences. Although they remained a point of historical novelty, they are often totally ignored in current psychology textbooks. In fact, few scholars give serious attention to the four temperament classifications, except as historical reference.

Nevertheless, the temperaments have been enjoying a revival outside of scientific circles. Neaman noted in 1975:

> Much degraded, but strangely influential, the traditions survive to our day in the popular forms of horoscopes and words like "sanguine," "choleric," "manic," "phlegmatic" and "melancholic." The modern world is experiencing a resurgence of interest in the relationship between genetics, birth seasons, physical traits and psychic dispositions.[22]

And nowhere are the four temperaments more popular than among astrologers and evangelical Christians.

The four temperaments evolved from a mythological, astrological view of man and the universe. They were consistently combined with the signs of the zodiac. They continue to be used to improve the human condition through knowing and tempering the strengths and weaknesses present at birth. Even though Christians who use the four temperaments today do so without the rest of astrology, the four temperaments are that feature of astrology made palatable for Christians.

3

Astrology
and the
Four Temperaments

Astrology is far more complex than the four temperaments. However, they actually belong together. From the early ideas of the four temperaments and through the Middle Ages, a person's temperament was believed to have been set according to the configurations of the sun, moon and planets. If a person was born under a particular sun sign, he would have a predetermined temperament.

The sun sign of a person pertains to the section of the zodiac the sun was passing through when the person was born. Although the sun sign is the major astrological sign related to a person's temperament, variations of the temperament also depend upon other configurations in the sky at the exact moment of birth. In fact, an astrologer casting a person's horoscope will interpret from 30 to 40 major factors along with 60 to 70 minor indicators.[1] Horoscopes can be extremely detailed. Thus, in addition to being born under the Gemini sign of the zodiac, for instance, and therefore being a type of Sanguine, other factors would bring in additional aspects of temperament. That is why horoscopes are cast for individuals.

The Four Temperaments and the Zodiac.

The twelve signs of the zodiac are arranged according to the elements (fire, earth, air, and water), the humors (yellow bile, black bile, blood, and phlegm), and the temperaments (choleric, melancholy, sanguine, and phlegmatic) three times round in sequence. The order is as follows:

Zodiac	Element	Humor	Temperament
Aries	Fire	Yellow Bile	Choleric
Taurus	Earth	Black Bile	Melancholy
Gemini	Air	Blood	Sanguine
Cancer	Water	Phlegm	Phlegmatic
Leo	Fire	Yellow Bile	Choleric
Virgo	Earth	Black Bile	Melancholy
Libra	Air	Blood	Sanguine
Scorpio	Water	Phlegm	Phlegmatic
Sagittarius	Fire	Yellow Bile	Choleric
Capricorn	Earth	Black Bile	Melancholy
Aquarius	Air	Blood	Sanguine
Pisces	Water	Phlegm	Phlegmatic

Thus there are three fire signs (Choleric), three earth signs (Melancholy), three air signs (Sanguine), and three water signs (Phlegmatic). The repetitions of three make up the fire triplicity, earth triplicity, air triplicity, and water triplicity. Each of the triplicities is identified with a temperament as well as with an element and a humor.

Aries, Leo, and Sagittarius make up the "fire triplicity." Astrologers teach that these signs manifest "different aspects of the Choleric temperament."[2] The Melancholy signs belong to the "earth triplicity," and they are Taurus, Virgo, and Capricorn.[3] Melancholy was thought to have come from "an excess of Earth element in the psychological make-up of the personality."[4]

The three zodiacal signs associated with the air element are Gemini, Libra, and Aquarius. These make up the "air triplicity," which is considered to manifest "different aspects of the Sanguine temperament." Notice how the following description of this triplicity matches a general Sanguine description:

> Since air was regarded as the most "restless" of the four elements, the three air signs were seen as being dominated by various degrees of restlessness and vacillation. . . .
>
> Each of the air signs is versatile and dedicated to human relationships, tending however to be lost in superficial and transient matters.[5]

Adjectives used to describe Gemini, for instance, are: "versatile, idealistic, communicative, imitative, inventive, alert, inquisitive. . . restless, impatient, unstable, superficial."[6] Adjectives often used to describe the Sanguine temperament are: sociable, outgoing, talkative, personable, friendly, lively, responsive, compassionate, carefree, restless, undisciplined.

The Phlegmatic signs belong to the "water triplicity" and they are Cancer, Scorpio, and Pisces.[7] The Phlegmatic temperament was thought to come from "an excess of the Water element in the psychological make-up of the personality."[8] Thus the temperaments were an integral part of astrology.

The four temperaments' connection to astrology is not accidental, but rather by original design. The temperament theories were built upon the same premises as astrology, and they were subsequently used together for many years. Even in the twentieth century, the four temperaments maintain their place in astrology.

It was only as various psychologists examined the four temperaments or drew from them to form their own personality theories and categories that the four temperaments have been treated as though they are independent from astrology. Nevertheless, while they may appear to stand on their own, the four temperaments are intrinsically part of astrology. They constitute an inadvertent way for people to practice an astrological kind of psychic and esoteric determinism without casting a horoscope and without even realizing that they are practicing the essence of astrology.

Problems with Astrology and the
Four Temperaments.

The problems of astrology addressed by Anker-berg and Weldon are also applicable to the practice of the four temperaments.[9] Neither astrology nor the four temperaments theory is scientific. Both are deceptive and invalid. Both reinterpret biblical doctrine. And both are bound to their occult roots.

While both astrology and the four temperaments have been subjected to scientific investigation, neither fulfills the requirements of science. Ankerberg and Weldon say, ". . . for a theory to be legitimate, the results must *have explanatory relevance* (the theory must explain something), and *be falsifiable* (i.e., be capable of being disproven)."[10] (Emphasis theirs.) They say that astrology does not meet these basic requirements. They continue:

> Modern astrology denies or rejects virtually every tenet of the scientific method: careful observation (observable cause and effect); critical appraisal; experimental testing; peer review (it can be demonstrated successfully to outsiders); explanatory relevance; falsifiability; causality; etc. . . . Concerning astrology, the indisputable conclusion is that the scientific evidence indicates that astrology fails at *everything* it claims to do.[11] (Emphasis theirs.)

The four temperaments constituent of astrology fails in the same regard.

Ankerberg and Weldon describe some studies conducted on astrology. They say:

> *The Mayo-White-Eysenck Study* attempted to determine if astrology could predict whether the personality of an adult would be introverted or extroverted. Over 2,300 adults had their extroversion/introversion scores tabulated on the Eysenck Personality Inventory (EPI), then these scores were correlated with astrological predictions.[12]

The results of the study were "marginal," meaning the results were slightly higher than chance. However, when five additional studies were conducted, only two supported the Mayo-White-Eysenck findings.[13] Ankerberg and Weldon report that in later research Eysenck himself concluded that "the entire astrological effect [of the original study] was due to the subjects' expectation and familiarity with the characteristics associated with their Zodiac signs."[14]

An interesting aspect of this study is that Eysenck's Personality Inventory has its own problems because of the highly subjective nature of introversion and extroversion. The same problems occur with the four temperaments. In fact, the four temperaments embody both the problems of astrological predictions of temperament and the problems of personality inventories, which we will discuss later.

Just as people could fit into various descriptions of the four temperament categories, they could fit into any one of the twelve zodiac signs. Ankerberg and Weldon say, "It is not uncommon to discover that a given astrological interpretation fits a subject perfectly, even though the chart is later discovered to be the wrong chart."[15]

They mention Dr. Marc Edmund Jones, who is both an ordained Presbyterian minister and "a leading astrologer in America." Jones admits that most astrological interpretations could "fit anybody, most of the time!"[16] Ankerberg and Weldon contend, "Astrology seems to work because astrologers make interpretations that are, or can be made, universally applicable."[17]

The seriousness of deception through astrology is so great that Ankerberg and Weldon say:

> Swindlers and practitioners of quack medicine are vigorously prosecuted by society because their deception and lies bring harm to people. Whether swindlers believe in their own scheme is irrelevant, for the public cannot and will not tolerate fraud. In its own sphere, astrology is a swindle, equivalent to quack medicine.[18]

The same can be said for that part of astrology known and promoted as the four temperaments. Sincere Christians who desire to help themselves and others are involved in a deception that has spiritual consequences.

Astrology has been connected with Babylon since before the Israelites were in bondage. However, God spoke to Babylon through His prophet

Isaiah. He said He would bring judgment upon them for this reason:

> For thou hast trusted in thy wickedness: thou hast said, None seeth me. Thy wisdom and thy knowledge, it hath perverted thee; and thou hast said in thine heart, I am, and none else beside me. Therefore shall evil come upon thee; thou shalt not know from whence it riseth: and mischief shall fall upon thee; thou shalt not be able to put it off: and desolation shall come upon thee suddenly, which thou shalt not know (Isaiah 47:10-11).

The Babylonians had trusted in themselves, but moreover they had trusted in esoteric knowledge and occult activities. Therefore, the Lord challenged them to find help in those evil, but futile exercises, and taunted them with these words :

> Stand now with thine enchantments, and with the multitude of thy sorceries, wherein thou hast laboured from thy youth; if so be thou shalt be able to profit, if so be thou mayest prevail. Thou art wearied in the multitude of thy counsels. Let now the astrologers, the stargazers, the monthly prognosticators, stand up, and save thee from these things that shall come upon thee (Isaiah 47:12-13).

Such practices belong to those who are in rebellion against God. They belong with the early stargazers who sought to build a tower to reach into the heavens. They do not belong to the Christian for whom Christ died and in whom the Holy Spirit dwells. Astrology is anathema to the Christian. And since the four temperaments are an intrinsic component of astrology, the four temperaments should be avoided as well.

While astrology is obviously occult and dangerous for Christians, there are some professing Christians who are involved in it. Ankerberg and Weldon tell the story of a minister who sought to fight the superstition of astrology. As part of his proof, he had his horoscope cast, but when it appeared accurate he was involved for eight years before he repented and turned to God for mercy.[19]

They describe another man who had been a Christian for 30 years, but who became interested in astrology through his interest in Carl Jung's works which "were filled with references to astrological symbolism." He confesses:

> Every day for 10 years I would rise and calculate my chart, my wife's and my children's. Instead of devoting time each day to prayer and Bible study, I was driven to involve myself in complicated astrological computations and interpretations. All the while, I sincerely felt that I was living my life according to God's will.[20]

How many Christians believe that they, too, are living their lives according to God's will, but are at the same time paying more attention to the four temperaments in relating to their families than to what the Lord's Word says about love and relationships? How many are attempting to improve themselves and others through the strengths and weaknesses of the four temperaments? How many are trying to shape their characters according to the four temperaments rather than remembering that it is God who is at work in each of His children. He is the one who is molding them into the image of Christ.

Faith in the Temperaments.

The four temperaments were part of the religious beliefs during Greek times. Along with the other practices of astrology and the worship of the sun, moon, and stars, there was the belief that there was a perfect balance of temperaments related to the esoteric fifth element. The *Dictionary of Astrology* says, "The astrological 'four elements' are actually five in number, the exoteric four being Earth, Air, Fire and Water, united by the fifth, which is the 'Quintessence.'"[21]

The four elements were considered to be unstable and in tension with each other. It was believed that the fifth, though not seen, keeps the other elements bound together, though never in perfect balance. Yet the Quintessence itself was thought to be the perfect balance.

In the same way, today's four temperaments believers are working towards that perfect balance of their temperament traits. There are the polarities pulling back and forth and the struggle to enhance the strengths and reduce the weaknesses. At the same time, as in astrology, there is a determinism that confines people to their temperament type. This is a faith system and a view of self in a cosmos of elements struggling against each other.

Even when combined with biblical teachings, the four temperaments do not become transformed. They are forever being tempered within the confines of determinism. True freedom does not come from figuring out one's temperament according to the relics of the four temperaments and astrology. Jesus already gave us the way to freedom, and that is through believing the Word of God and living by that Truth (John 8:31-32).

True freedom does not even come from learning the four temperaments and then redefining the fruit of the Spirit into so-called temperament traits of the new nature. The four temperaments are rooted in paganism and astrology. **Christians do not need pagan beliefs and practices, such as the four temperaments, to grow spiritually. If they did, the Bible would have included such teachings.** The four temperaments were certainly available at the time, along with all the other pagan practices that were an abomination to God. Instead of incorporating the Greek teachings of the humors and temperaments for self-improvement, Paul insisted that there is only one true Gospel and that "the hope of glory" is "Christ in you."

Paul's Warning.

The apostle Paul warned: "Beware lest any man spoil you through philosophy and vain deceit, after the tradition of men, after the rudiments of the world, and not after Christ" (Colossians 2:8). His warning may have included a direct reference to the rudiments of astrology and the four temperaments. Two basic concepts having to do with the early Greek astrologers were "principles" and "elements." Astrologers followed the Aristotelian belief that four principles ruled matter.

As described earlier, the principles were hot, cold, moist and dry and the four elements were fire, earth, water, and air. The principles were thought to rule matter through interacting as pairs of opposites. The *Dictionary of Astrology* explains:

> These were the pairs of interacting opposites said to underlie all phenomena: the hot and moist united forms and brought increase—the dry and cold separated form and brought destruction. The polarities, or "principles" . . . . played a most important part in early astrological doctrine.[22]

They also played a major role in medicine's attempts to balance the body's humors.

The Greek word for "elements" is *stoicheion*. It is also translated as "elementary principles." Thus the same word could be used to denote the basic elements (fire, air, earth, water) and the underlying principles of their corresponding elements (hot, cold, dry, and moist). When used in the plural, *stoicheion* "primarily signifies any first things from which others in a series, or a composite whole, take their rise."[23] These meanings may have a direct bearing on Colossians 2:8, in which Paul warns against "philosophies," "vain deceits," and the "rudiments of the world." The word translated "rudiments" or "elementary principles" in Colossians 2:8 is that same word *stoicheion*.

Concerning the word *stoicheion*, *The Expanded Vine's Expository Dictionary of the New Testament* says:

> In the N.T. it is used of (*a*) the substance of the material world, 2 Pet. 3:10, 12; (*b*) the delusive speculations of Gentile cults and of Jewish theories, treated as elementary principles, "the rudiments of the world," Col. 2:8, spoken of as "philosophy and vain deceit;" these were presented as superior to faith in Christ; at Colossae the worship of angels, mentioned in ver. 18, is explicable by the supposition, held by both Jews and Gentiles in that district, that the constellations were either themselves animated heavenly beings, or were governed by them.[24]

Thus, in the very same word lie the possibilities of the Greek teachings on the four elements and the four principles. Therefore, the *stoicheion* spoken of by Paul may, indeed, have been those "first principles" of Empedocles and Hippocrates (hot, cold, moist, and dry) as related to the elements (earth, air, fire, and water).

Moreover, the apostle Paul may also have been warning against those principles and elements as they related to the four temperaments and astrology. Could it be that Paul was specifically including the Greek philosophies of the four elements, the four principles or qualities, the four temperaments, and astrology in his warning? Indeed, the subject of worshiping angels in the same passage may be related to the occult significance of the four elements—earth, air, fire, and water—as they went beyond physical compounds of the earth and were thought of as spirit beings in themselves.

In using the word *stoicheion*, which can be translated "elementary principles" and "elements," which are basic to the four temperaments, Paul could actually have been warning against astrology and the four temperaments, along with other philosophies and vain deceits. No doubt he was familiar with Greek teachings of humors, temperaments, and other aspects of astrology.

Even if Paul had not been familiar with such teachings, they nevertheless would fit into the general category of "philosophies," "vain deceits," and "rudiments of the world." Paul urged Christians to continue their walk with the Lord on the same basis as their initial salvation. He wrote:

> As ye have therefore received Christ Jesus the Lord, so walk ye in him: Rooted and built up in him, and stablished in the faith, as ye have been taught, abounding therein with thanksgiving. Beware lest any man spoil you through philosophy and vain

> deceit, after the tradition of men, after the
> rudiments of the world, and not after
> Christ. For in him dwelleth all the fulness
> of the Godhead bodily. And ye are complete
> in him, which is the head of all principality
> and power (Colossians 2:6-10).

Then after he completed his warnings in Chapter 2
of Colossians, he said:

> If ye then be risen with Christ, seek those
> things which are above, where Christ
> sitteth on the right hand of God. Set your
> affection on things above, not on things on
> the earth. For ye are dead, and your life is
> hid with Christ in God (Colossians 3:1-3).

Such an admonition certainly encourages
Christians to change the direction of their focus
from self and the things of the world to the Lord
and His promises and provisions. Why would
anyone need to be bound to a temperament
category—forever struggling with their so-called
temperaments, when they are complete in Christ?
Indeed, the four temperament teachings, rather
than encouraging spiritual growth, can actually
interfere with God's work in a believer's life. Why
not leave the temperaments with astrology and
"press toward the mark for the prize of the high
calling of God in Christ Jesus" (Philippians 3:14).

4

Temperament Teachers

Numerous Christians believe in and promote the four temperaments as a means of understanding human nature and behavior. The two most prolific promoters are Dr. Tim LaHaye and Florence Littauer. Their books and seminars have touched and influenced millions of Christians. More than anyone else, they can be credited with having enticed Christians into understanding and explaining themselves and others in terms of Sanguine, Choleric, Melancholy, and Phlegmatic.

Throughout their books, each author presents lists of traits and characteristics which they think are typical of the various temperaments and types. And each provides easy ways to figure out who is what. Everyone can be fit into a four-fold temperament classification by having universal characteristics listed for each of the four types. Then, since the characteristics are applicable to everyone to one

degree or another, everyone can find himself somewhere. To make it easy, everyone can be a combination of types so that no one has to fit perfectly
anywhere. One could feasibly concoct almost any
combination and people could fit themselves and
others into the compartments. That's one reason
typologies are so popular.

The temperament promoters sincerely believe
in what they are doing. LaHaye contends that "it is
essential to know your temperament and to be able
to analyze other people's temperaments."[1] He
further testifies that "of all the behavior theories
ever devised, it [the four temperaments theory] has
served as the most helpful explanation."[2]

LaHaye and others make strong declarations
about the importance of understanding ourselves
and others through their categories. They also
make promises and wild claims about their systems' fantastic results. Marriages and children
flourish, they claim. Great success is just around
the corner. LaHaye believes it is important to
determine one's basic temperament type to discover
one's "potential strengths and weaknesses." Thus,
he offers what he calls a "program for overcoming
your weaknesses through the power of God in
you."[3]

LaHaye's Temperament System.

LaHaye introduced the four temperaments to
evangelical Christians in 1966. The four temperaments had virtually been discarded after the
Middle Ages and discounted as a valid means of

understanding people, until a few lone souls discovered them among relics of the past and marketed them in twentieth-century language. One of those lone souls was Dr. Ole Hallesby, a Norwegian theologian who wrote *Temperamentene i kristelig lys*, published in 1940 and translated into English in 1962 as *Temperament and the Christian Faith*.[4] LaHaye says he "drew extensively" from *Temperament and the Christian Faith* in writing his book *Spirit-Controlled Temperament*, which was published four years after the English translation of Hallesby's book.[5]

Hallesby's book has no footnote references to undergird his statements about each of the four temperaments. Therefore, his book is a combination of his own limited observations and the opinions of other unnamed individuals. Nevertheless, as he discusses the characteristics of a Sanguine, Choleric, Melancholy, or Phlegmatic person, he speaks as though what he says is fact. LaHaye follows in the same tradition. Although he does credit Hallesby for much of his material, he has no research or other support for the detailed delineation of characteristics. The categories and descriptions have been passed down through the ages in the same way as old wives' tales, against which Scripture clearly warns (1 Timothy 4:7).

LaHaye also drew from the book *Fact and Fiction in Psychology* by English psychologist Dr. Hans Eysenck, who was interested in investigating the four temperaments as well as astrology. Eysenck attempted to use the basic four temperaments categories to distinguish individual differences among people as they relate to emotional stability and neuroticism.[6] Having drawn from various writers of earlier centuries, he assigned traits to the four temperament categories and had numerous individuals rate themselves and others according to those traits. He then added additional dimensions of "Unstable" and "Stable" and "Introverted" and "Extraverted" and came up with the following circle:

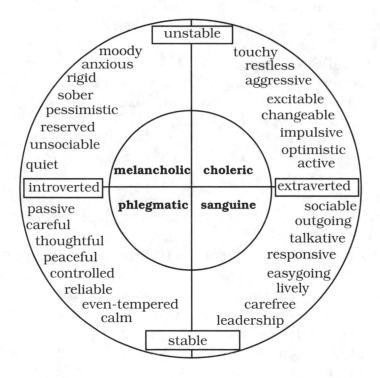

In Eysenck's circle of temperaments the Choleric and Melancholic quadrants are toward the "Unstable," and the Sanguine and Phlegmatic are toward the "Stable." The Sanguine and Choleric are on the "Extraverted" side of the circle and the Melancholic and Phlegmatic are on the "Introverted" side.[7]

Eysenck's extensive research was hampered by subjectivity. Both the reporting and the self-reporting scales were based on subjective evaluations limited to items on the questionnaires or tests. Though he developed an interesting personality inventory and conducted extensive research, the very subjectivity of his work prevented it from being considered seriously even among members of his own profession.

Several discrepancies can be seen by comparing LaHaye's and Eysenck's descriptions. For instance, while Eysenck identifies the word *unstable* with the Melancholic and the Choleric, LaHaye uses the word *unstable* to define the Sanguine.[8] LaHaye also revised Eysenck's circle of temperaments to show the "strengths" and "weaknesses" of each temperament.

LaHaye changed and rearranged some of the descriptive terms as well. While there are some similarities between Eysenck's and LaHaye's descriptions of the four temperaments, there are enough discrepancies to illustrate the fact that they are not dealing with objective fact. Descriptions and lists of characteristics for each of the four temperaments vary from person to person. The entire business of describing the four temperaments and assigning people to categories is such a subjective act that it is both useless and misleading.

LaHaye continued to promote the defunct four temperaments in his book *Transformed Temperaments*. In that book he makes several errors regarding the history of the four temperaments. He apparently did not understand the depth and extent of the work by Claudius Galen of Pergamum in the delineation of the characteristics of the four temperaments. Moreover, he mistakenly says that Galen lived in the 17th rather than the second century.[9] While this may seem inconsequential, it reveals the lack of solid research conducted in preparation for a book that purports to tell people how to utilize the four temperaments theory of personality for the purpose of spiritual growth.

LaHaye seems to have used minimal resources for his descriptions of the four temperaments. He primarily drew from Ole Hallesby's book (which is totally devoid of academic references or research) and quotes from the German philosopher, Immanuel Kant, as recorded in Eysenck's book *Fact and Fiction in Psychology*.[10] LaHaye surely could not have taken the rest of Eysenck's book seriously or he would have come up with somewhat different categories and would have been far more cautious in his pronouncements about the wholesale use of the four temperaments for spiritual growth.

In spite of LaHaye's declaration that "the four-fold classification of temperaments is still widely used," psychological theorists had generally abandoned the four temperaments typology. In fact, it is difficult to find recent academic material dealing with the four temperaments. Aside from their historical value, the four temperaments have all but disappeared from the research scene as antiquated, out-dated means of analyzing and understanding human nature. As for validation with external criteria, it is interesting that LaHaye would attempt to validate the temperament theory on the basis of handwriting experts.[11] These graphologists claim that a person's handwriting reveals his personality. However, numerous research studies have refuted their claims.[12]

LaHaye can be commended for criticizing the influence of Sigmund Freud and for the way Freud's deterministic theories undermine personal responsibility. However, the four temperaments theory of personality has its own responsibility escape hatch: "I was born that way—that's my temperament—therefore I can't help the way I am." And though Christians who promote the four temperaments notions would not want the system to work that way, it does anyway. A great deal of behavior is "understood" and thereby excused on the basis of temperament traits.

LaHaye can also be commended for his concern over the way "much of the world today worships before the shrine of psychology and psychiatry."[13] And, indeed that is even more evident today than when he wrote those words. However, the four temperaments theory of personality is among the worst kinds of psychology. Furthermore, it is a means of opening Christians to other psychological theories dressed in Bible verses. Those who integrate the four temperaments theory of personality are doing the same thing as those who integrate any other personality theory with Christianity, be it Freud's, Jung's, Adler's, Maslow's, Rogers', Hippocrates', Galen's, or Kant's.

Just as Freud believed that man is driven by unseen forces in his unconscious, LaHaye teaches that a person's temperament is "the unseen force underlying human action." He says:

> There is nothing more fascinating about man than his temperament! It is tempera-ment that provides each human being with the distinguishing qualities of uniqueness that make him as individually different from his fellowmen as the differing designs God has given to snowflakes. It is the un-seen force underlying human action, a force that can destroy a normal and productive human being unless it is disciplined and directed.[14]

Immediately one assumes that understanding one's temperament is essential if one is to escape destruction and become productive.

LaHaye uses the following descriptions of the four temperaments in his 1966 book:

Positive Traits	**Negative Traits**
SANGUINE	
Enjoying	Restless
Optimistic	Weak-Willed
Friendly	Egotistical
Compassionate	Emotionally Unstable

CHOLERIC

Strong Will Power	Hot-Tempered
Practical	Cruel
Leader	Impetuous
Optimistic	Self-Sufficient

MELANCHOLY

Sensitive	Self-Centered
Perfectionist	Pessimistic
Analytical	Moody
Faithful Friend	Revengeful
Self-Sacrificing	

PHLEGMATIC

Witty	Slow and Lazy
Dependable	Tease
Practical	Stubborn
Efficient	Indecisive[15]

LaHaye also includes Carl Jung's Introvert-Extrovert typology in his scheme and places the Sanguine and Choleric under the Extrovert type and the Melancholy and Phlegmatic under the Introvert type.[16] He also assigns the "universal sin" of anger to the Sanguine and Choleric and the "universal sin" of fear to the Melancholy and Phlegmatic.[17] The charts and descriptions make the whole set-up look factual and reliable. However, these are arbitrary classifications and combinations. Throughout his later books he adds and embellishes the lists and even makes up a test that people can take to fit themselves into his system.

LaHaye lays the usual groundwork of temperament strengths and weaknesses, combines them with Scripture and comes up with a foreign paradigm of man's sinful nature and sanctification process. He begins Chapter One of *Spirit-Controlled Temperament* with, "Why is it that I can't control myself?" He then quotes Romans 7:18-20 and says, "The 'sin' that dwelled in him was the natural weaknesses that he, like all human beings, inherited from his parents."[18] He continues:

> We have all inherited a basic temperament from our parents that contains both strengths and weaknesses. This temperament is called several things in the Bible, "the natural man," "the flesh," "the old man," and "corruptible flesh," to name a few. It is the basic impulse of our being that seeks to satisfy our wants.[19]

LaHaye then attempts to distinguish between temperament, character, and personality. He defines *temperament* as "the combination of inborn traits that subconsciously affects man's behavior." He calls *character* "the real you" and equates it with "the hidden man of the heart" and the soul. He contends that character "is the result of your natural temperament modified by childhood training, education, and basic attitudes, beliefs, principles, and motivations." Finally, he defines *personality* as "the outward expression of our-

selves," which may be "the same as our character"
or simply "a pleasing facade for an unpleasant or
weak character."[20] LaHaye concludes:

> In summary, temperament is the combina-
> tion of traits we were born with; character
> is our "civilized" temperament; and person-
> ality is the "face" we show to others.[21]

While he desires to present a biblical anthropology,
LaHaye arbitrarily presents his definition of man
in terms of psychological opinion, rather than in
terms of biblical categories.

LaHaye insists that temperament is genetic.
However, in the first paragraph of Chapter One in
his book *Why You Act the Way You Do*, he tells this
story:

> When I was in high school there was a pair
> of identical twins in my class. We could
> hardly tell them apart. They tested out
> identically on their IQ scores (128). But
> that is where the similarities stopped. One
> was personable; the other withdrew from
> people. One loved sports, history, and liter-
> ature; the other preferred math, physics,
> and language. Interesting to me was the
> fact that their grade-point averages were
> almost identical at the end of their four
> years in high school. Yet they did not get
> the same grades in most subjects. What
> made the difference between these young
> men? Their temperaments![22]

Such a story does not support a genetic theory of temperaments, because according to the genetic theory the twins would have the same temperament. The story contradicts the theory. And that is typical of temperament theories. There are lots of contradictions because there are lots of presuppositions that have not been validated by any truly objective measure.

Lots of assumptions are made and presented as truth, when in fact much is simply myth. Which myth will you believe? That Phlegmatics are fat and lazy (the usual erroneous assumption) or that they rarely gain weight because they eat slowly and deliberately[23] (LaHaye's unproven assumption)? That the best students are Cholerics because of their need to achieve or the Melancholies because of their inquisitive minds? That Phlegmatics are born procrastinators or that they are the only temperament type to pay their bills early?

LaHaye equates temperament with our "old nature." He says, "Since temperament is our 'old nature,' what man needs is a 'new nature.'"[24] But LaHaye does not teach that the temperament is to be reckoned dead or put off as the old man is to be reckoned dead and put off. He only seems to want to put off the "weaknesses," which he calls "sin." He wants to keep and enhance the "strengths."

In Scripture, the old nature is the sinful nature, referred to as the "old man." If our temperament is equivalent to our old nature, it would thereby have to be be reckoned dead and put off (Romans 6:6-11; Ephesians 4:22; Colossians 3:9). If the temperament is the "old nature," both strengths and weaknesses would need to be reckoned dead and put off.

Further confusion arises when LaHaye boldly declares:

> Once you have determined your basic temperament, pay close attention to your strengths and weaknesses. It is not God's will that your natural traits be destroyed.[25]

Such confusion arises from attempting to wed a pagan system of "strengths" and "weaknesses"—the four temperaments' astrological polarities—with biblical doctrines of man. One does not need to delve into pagan philosophies and the "rudiments of this world" to discover one's talents or one's temptations to sin.

Since LaHaye believes that temperament traits are genetic and permanent, he says, "Temperament traits, whether controlled or uncontrolled, last throughout life." Yet on the same page he contends that there is a way to change one's temperament.[26] And, the way he says that a person can change his temperament is through becoming a new creature in Christ. With a simple shift from the ideas and categories of human conception to biblical doctrines and categories, LaHaye turns temperament (one of the four temperaments or combination thereof) into our "old nature." Then, by a huge leap of the imagination, he turns the nine fruit of the Spirit from Galatians 5 into "temperament traits" of our new nature.[27]

There are a number of problems with such an equation, one being that according to Colossians we are to put off the old and put on the new (3:9-10), which would not fit into what he proposes throughout his book. He wants us to control our old nature (natural temperament) with the "temperament traits" of our new nature. In other words, he is proposing a two-nature cooperation or compromise. That is quite different from putting the old man to death according to Romans 6 and walking in the Spirit according to Romans 8.

Furthermore, people who try to wed the four temperaments (or any other such personality types) with Scripture emphasize strengths and weaknesses of each type rather than obedience and disobedience to God. One person may be more prone to sin in one area than in another and individual differences do exist. But, to attempt to deal with these differences through a four temperaments typology undermines the Holy Spirit's work in a person's life. Psychological systems for explaining and understanding man's essence tend to replace relationship with the Lord Jesus with formulas and techniques.

Nevertheless, LaHaye contends that the four temperaments theory of understanding humanity is compatible with the Bible. He says:

> The four temperaments seem to appeal to Christians because they are so compatible with many scriptural concepts. Just as the Bible teaches that all men have a sinful nature, the temperaments teach that all

men have weaknesses. The Bible teaches that man has a besetting sin, and the temperaments highlight it. The Bible says man has "an old nature" which is the "flesh" or "corruptible flesh." Temperament is made up of inborn traits, some of which are weaknesses.[28]

Then, since the Bible does not directly teach the four temperaments, LaHaye presents four major persons from the Bible in terms of the temperaments. LaHaye warns people about indiscriminately using the four temperament classifications on others.[29] Nevertheless, he audaciously presumes to apply the four temperaments to Peter, Paul, Moses, and Abraham in *Transformed Temperaments*. He turns Peter into a Sanguine, Paul into a Choleric, Moses into a Melancholy, and Abraham into a Phlegmatic.[30]

In his book *Why You Act the Way You Do*, LaHaye turns King David into a combination of Sanguine and Melancholy.[31] But, another teacher of the four temperaments, Florence Littauer, says that when people seem to have opposite temperaments, such as Sanguine and Melancholy, one of the temperaments is actually a mask.

Littauer says, "God didn't create us with antagonistic personalities in one body."[32] Then she quotes James 1:8, "A double-minded man is unstable in all his ways." Does that mean King David, a man after God's own heart, wore a mask and was double-minded and unstable in all his ways? To arbitrarily plop an historical figure into a category

is nonsense. It leads to a distortion of that historical person and distracts from the biblical intent. It
also gives the impression that people can arbitrarily and authoritatively be assigned to one of the four
temperament types.

When reading the various extended descriptions of the various temperaments, one can see that
much has been added and assumed since ancient
times. But who can object to the creative addition of
all kinds of details and predictions of each of the
temperaments and how they will act in various
circumstances? If one were to read several of these
books by different authors at one sitting, one might
notice that contradictions and silliness abound.

To his credit, one of LaHaye's goals for teaching
the temperaments is to encourage people to be
filled with the Spirit and have the Holy Spirit
control and transform their natural temperament.[33]
And, rather than simply calling the temperament
weaknesses *weaknesses*, he does talk about sin in
reference to them.[34] Nevertheless, concentration on
the temperament types can easily become a hindrance rather than a help. There is no Scriptural
justification for using a pagan system to encourage
spiritual growth.

That using the temperaments is totally unnecessary can be seen in the story of a man who had
been transformed by the Spirit even though he did
not know that he had previously been a "typical,
fire-eating   Choleric   with   some   melancholy
tendencies."[35] LaHaye himself gives this example:

This man knew nothing about temperament, but he did know what it was to be
filled with the Holy Spirit. So it isn't essential to know the principles of temperament
to be modified by the Holy Spirit, but such
principles will point up the greatest areas
of weaknesses in our lives so we can **speed
up the process of modification.**[36] (Emphasis added.)

Indeed, he did not have to know about the four temperaments. The Christian does not need pagan
knowledge to "speed up the process of modification." God has already given him all he needs for
the process of sanctification.

While one of the ostensible reasons for using
the temperament theory is to help us see our
weaknesses and sins so that we overcome them, the
Holy Spirit does not need extrabiblical theory to
point out sin. Because of the system's pagan nature
and the errors involved, a Christian may come into
the bondage of trying to fix himself up through
modifying his weaknesses and exercising his
strengths, rather than allowing the Holy Spirit to
work in His way.

If we truly want to identify our besetting sins
and our sinful habits, the Lord will give us ample
opportunity to discover them. Our problem is not
that we cannot discover our sinful tendencies without knowing the four temperaments. Our problem
is not wanting to notice our own sinfulness. But
when we are ready, the Lord is faithful to answer
such a prayer as Psalm 139:23-24.

Search me, O God, and know my heart: try
me, and know my thoughts:
And see if there be any wicked way in me,
and lead me in the way everlasting.

Littauer's Temperament System.

Florence Littauer followed in LaHaye's steps
after reading his book *Spirit-Controlled Temperament.*[37] Since that time she has conducted seminars
and written a number of books focused on personality types. In her delightful manner and amusing
anecdotes, Littauer easily entices Christians into
the temperament mentality. She encourages self-
analysis through understanding and applying the
four temperaments, because she believes that such
knowledge can help people truly become what God
intended them to be—that they can reach their full
potential. She says:

> Do you know that God wants to use your
> personality, your background, your abili-
> ties, your gifts for his Glory? He created
> you for such a time as this, but he wants
> you to know who you really are so that you
> will be a genuine and sincere person, not
> one hiding behind a mask of confusion.[38]

Rather than focusing on our identity in Christ,
Littauer contends that we must know our temperament. Thus, she outlines the four temperaments
and provides a personality test so that we can all
discover who we really are. Evidently the Lord and

His Word are not sufficient to guide us into knowing who we are and becoming the persons God
intends us to be. Otherwise there would be no need
for her to add the ancient temperament tool, rooted
in Greek philosophy, astrology, and mythology.

Littauer believes in the utter importance of the
four temperaments. She says:

> In these times of global tension and inner
> turmoil, I find so many Christian people
> who are longing for some sense of identity
> and self-worth, some answers to their frus-
> trations and searchings. . . . They study the
> Word; they know they are created in God's
> image and made slightly lower than the
> angels; they've been crucified in Christ and
> have taken off the old clothes and put on
> the new. They've gone to church, knelt at
> the altar on Sunday, and taught Bible stud-
> ies. In spite of all these positive spiritual
> steps, they still need some simple solution
> to who they really are as individuals.[39]

Evidently "all spiritual blessings in heavenly
places in Christ" (Ephesians 1:3) and "all things
that pertain unto life and godliness, through the
knowledge of Him" (2 Peter 1:3) are not enough for
the modern Christian. Apparently God now needs
the help of the pagan system of temperaments. According to Littauer, God is the one who is using the
four temperaments. She says that she is "amazed
at how God uses this tool to open people's eyes to
themselves and their relationships with others."[40]

Evidently, for some people, putting off the old and putting on the new life in Jesus is not enough. They need to know their temperament.[41] Littauer explains that when they, as branches, were connected to the vine, Jesus Christ, they were "not connected with what [they] were originally intended to be"[42] if they "unconsciously stifled [their] natural traits . . . to please a parent or partner."[43] She warns that a person may be wearing a false temperament mask, especially if he identifies with a temperament which is the opposite from what others would identify as his true temperament.

This is so serious a problem that Littauer declares, "We will never reach the potential that is within us until we pull off the mask and become the real person God intended us to be."[44] And by that she is referring to a temperament mask that can only be removed by understanding what temperament we actually are.

In adopting and adapting the temperament types, some of the current enthusiasts ignore the fact that the Greeks, Romans, and medieval Europeans sought to temper the temperaments. They believed that physical and mental health came from blending the four elements and humors so that a perfect balance would be reached. Yet, Littauer teaches that if a person is not definitely one type or a strong combination of two types he probably does not know who he is. In fact, he may have real problems. She teaches that if a person is a seeming blend of opposite types, he is probably wearing a personality mask, does not know who he is, and no doubt has serious problems.[45]

Littauer is so adamant about the importance of self-knowledge concerning temperament traits that she gives a new command in this rhetorical question:

> If we come prepackaged with certain blendings of our parents' personalities, isn't it our duty to the Lord to be as true to our basic traits as we possibly can?[46]

Is it really "our duty to the Lord to be as true to our basic traits as we possibly can?" Where is the Scriptural justification? Of course we are not to be dishonest or deceptive, but to be "as true to our basic traits as we possibly can" is not presented as a duty in the Bible—not in the Ten Commandments nor in the Great Commandment to love God nor in the Second, to love neighbor as self. One gets the distinct impression that the commandments of men are being added to the Word of God and presented as God's will.

From Littauer's manner in presenting the four types, it appears that she believes God meant each person to be one of the four temperament types. She introduces each one with the following questions:

> Were you **meant to be** a Sanguine?. . .
> Were you **meant to be** a Choleric?. . .
> Were you **meant to be** a Melancholy?. . .
> Were you **meant to be** a Phlegmatic?. . .[47]
> (Emphasis added.)

Certainly God created humanity with individual differences, but He did not create the four temperament categories.

If the four temperaments theory of personality were biblical, such descriptive categories would have been developed in Scripture, at least to some degree. For instance, Scripture clearly delineates between the Gentiles and the Jews, between the saved and the lost, and between the flesh and the spirit. Such categories are not simply hinted at or creatively drawn out of a few verses. Chapters and entire books are devoted to distinguishing between believers and unbelievers and between walking after the flesh or according to the Spirit. Therefore, if there is to be another system for understanding the dynamics of personality and behavior, one should expect as clear a presentation in Scripture, if, indeed, it is one to be followed by Christians.

Instead of originating from Scripture or following clearly designated biblical categories, those who enthusiastically promote temperament theories, personality profiles and other typologies are introducing foreign paradigms which originated in paganism. Once such foreign paradigms are introduced, they are used to understand and explain the human condition undergirded by a new interpretation of Scripture.

Littauer's goal is similar to all purveyors of temperament types and signs of the zodiac. She says:

> Our aim in studying the temperaments is to assess our basic strengths and realize

that we are people of value and worth; to
become aware of our weaknesses and set
out to overcome them to learn that just
because other people are different doesn't
make them wrong; and to accept the fact
that since we can't change them, we might
as well love them as they are.[48]

Aspects of this goal sound worthy: to make use of
our capabilities, to overcome weaknesses, to notice
that not all people are alike, to realize that we
cannot change other people, and to love them
anyway. However, one does not have to have ever
read descriptions of temperament types to reach
such a goal.

As a matter of fact, when a person follows the
temperament path to the goal he may actually miss
what God has for him. He may emphasize the
capabilities that are secondary to God's plan for his
life; he may "overcome weaknesses" without ever
dying to self; he may put people into boxes to
manage their differences; and he may maintain
sentimental, gushy feelings without the inconve-
nience of sacrificial love.

Littauer claims that many people have found
freedom to be themselves through her teachings.
After one such testimonial, she says:

The study of the temperaments is not a
theology but a tool to understanding ourselves and learning to get along with
others.[49]

Immediately after that she quotes John 8:36 (NIV): "If the Son sets you free, you will be free indeed." Does she think that her teachings are as important or equal to the words of Jesus? John 8:36 must be read in context. Jesus was talking about His Word and the disciples following and continuing in His Word. That is the Truth that sets people free, not the pagan teachings of the four temperaments!

Littauer's system promises that besides being free to be oneself, an individual will know how to get his own unique-to-his-temperament needs met. She says:

> Without an understanding of the basic temperaments and the desires and needs of each, we tend to spend much of our time trying to get from other people responses that they just can't give.[50]

She then presents the emotional needs unique to each temperament:

Sanguine	Choleric	Melancholy	Phlegmatic
attention	achievement	sensitivity	respect
approval	appreciation	order	feeling of worth[51]

This is especially important, because she says that if their needs are not met, they are vulnerable to temptation.[52] This reveals how the unbiblical need psychology of such humanistic psychologists as Alfred Adler, Abraham Maslow, and Carl Rogers influences the purveyors of typologies.

While speculation abounds in four temperaments theories and presentations, there is one
certainty: there will be an abundance of promises
and a torrent of testimonies to match them. Promises are made that you will understand yourself
and reach your highest potential and overcome
your weaknesses. You will also be able to understand and overcome depression.[53] You will be able
to be true to you, whatever that may mean—
depending upon whether you are being true to your
"strengths" or true to your "weaknesses." Furthermore, all of us can be leaders if we understand our
own temperament. Littauer promises:

> We can all be leaders no matter what our
> background, education or personality, if we
> can find a way to assess our abilities and
> learn to eliminate our negatives.[54]

> Whichever personality you may have, you
> can be a leader. As you accept your
> strengths and talents and work to over-
> come your weaknesses, you will grow into
> your limitless potential and become the
> leader you were meant to be.[55]

Who can argue with a system that has such
great success—at least according to its enthusiasts?
Littauer claims that after informally introducing
the temperament tool to a small group of people,
"We saw in one week's time a new understanding
between husbands and wives, a release of tension
and self-judgment, and a new freedom to be what

God wanted each one to be."[56] With such promotion and enthusiasm, who can resist?

Concerning the four temperaments, Littauer claims that "their usefulness and validity remain the same today as they were in ancient Greece."[57] If that were the case, psychologists and psychiatrists would not have given up on the four temperaments years ago. If that were the case, people would not have spent centuries revising, renaming, and restructuring ways to understand people. And, if that were the case, there would be evidence beyond the flimsy, nonvalid personality tests people use to sustain typology myths.

Furthermore, if "their usefulness and validity remain the same today as they were in ancient Greece," they are still pagan systems of knowing who man is and why he behaves the way he does. They are still as useful and valid as the horoscope.

Littauer quotes a letter from one of her fans, who naively saw the connection between the horoscope and the four temperaments. She wrote, "I believe your temperament study may possibly be God's answer to the 'horror-scope.' When someone mentions his 'sign,' I explain the temperaments."[58] Little does the letter writer realize that they are from the same source and basically the same.

Saying the four temperaments "may possibly be God's answer to the 'horror-scope'" is equivalent to saying Buddhism may be God's answer to "Hindyism." Littauer admits:

> The one overwhelming conclusion I've come to is that no matter what the traits are

labeled, they all seem to spring from the
same rootstock of Hippocrates' theory of the
humors.[59]

Yes, and that rootstock is pagan astrology.

Scripture does not set forth a system of personality differences, but rather one of putting off the
old self and putting on the new; of loving God and
following His way rather than the way of the self; of
loving one another sacrificially as we already love
ourselves. No matter what the individual differences are between people, love is the issue and obedience to the Lord is the response.

Understanding ourselves in terms of typologies
is unnecessary for walking after the Spirit and
bearing the fruit of the Spirit. Concentration on
such categories only feeds the flesh and ultimately
leads to works of the flesh. Focusing on temperament and personality categories, profiles, and tests
avoids the real problem of sin and attempts to fix
us up with the ways of the world.

5

Personality
DiSCovery?

Ken Voges and Ron Braund, authors of *Understanding How Others Misunderstand You*, have
joined ranks with the popularizers of personality
types. Rather than using ancient categories from
the Greeks, they use the DiSC model developed by
William Marston. Voges had previously used the
four temperaments promoted by LaHaye and
Littauer.[1] However, when he discovered the DiSC
model, he eagerly embraced it. He says:

> But when I came into contact with John
> Geier's refinement of the DiSC material
> popularized by William Marston, it was
> evident that Geier and Marston had come
> up with a more comprehensive explanation
> of personality traits than the four-tempera-
> ment model.[2]

Besides being a revised and updated version of the four temperaments, the DiSC model is accompanied by the *Personal Profile System*,[3] an instrument for classifying people according to the following behavior styles: "Dominance," "Influencing," Steadiness," "Compliance."[4]

Voges liked the *Personal Profile System* and saw great potential for its use among Christians. In fact he enjoyed categorizing people with the DiSC model so much that he used it to analyze and classify men and women from the Bible. He says:

> Since others [e.g. LaHaye] had done some initial association of temperaments with biblical characters, I cross-referenced that material to the DiSC materials and carried out my own study of the Scriptures.[5]

Thus he admits to using an extrabiblical paradigm by which to study and interpret Scripture. When one remembers the four temperaments' roots, modifications and revisions, one has to conclude that this extrabiblical paradigm is pagan—wedded to all of man's ways to live without God. Yet, this is now a Bible study tool, eagerly embraced by Christians who should know better.

After his extensive "Bible study" with the DiSC paradigm, Voges devised the *Biblical Personal Profile*, an inventive marketing device to inspire the faith of Christians. He then joined with the DiSC people to promote his *Biblical Personal Profile* together with the secular *Personal Profile System*. The end result is a scientific-sounding, unbiblical

four temperaments model for understanding people
plus a biblical facade painted with Bible characters
molded to fit the DiSC categories.

In an attempt to make paganistic and worldly
systems of temperament theories and personality
profiles appear biblical, the promoters attempt to
analyze and classify various biblical characters.
Personality types and individual differences are
presented to explain the actions of such people as
Moses, David, Paul, and even Jesus.

Voges and Braund boldly assert that Joshua
was a High D (Dominant), since that would have to
be the personality type of someone who could lead
the Israelite army. Then they say:

> In order to keep Joshua from becoming
> overconfident in his ability to lead, God
> gave him an important personal assign-
> ment: to meditate on "the Book of the Law"
> "day and night" so that he would be able to
> follow God's leading (Joshua 1:8).[6]

But, did God direct Joshua to meditate on the
Law of God to overcome a particular personality
weakness? Or does the Law of God have to do with
sin and righteousness? Joshua was to meditate on
the Law of God so that he would know it thoroughly
in order to lead the Israelites. There is no indica-
tion in Scripture that God told Joshua that he had
a personality weakness of being overconfident. All
of Joshua's confidence recorded in Scripture had to
do with his faith in God. After all, he had accompanied Moses to Mount Sinai and had seen God's

power. Joshua's confidence was in the Lord, not in himself. Voges and Braund's reasoning is absurd. It undermines Scripture.

Voges and Braund also identify Sarah as a High D (Dominant) personality. They say that Sarah "argued for a new approach to achieving their goal"[7] to have a child. The biblical record doesn't even hint at an argument from a dominant personality. The attitude seems to be one of supplication:

> And Sarai said unto Abram, Behold now, the LORD hath restrained me from bearing: I pray thee, go in unto my maid; it may be that I may obtain children by her. And Abram hearkened to the voice of Sarai (Genesis 16:2).

Sarah is the biblical example of submission, not dominance.

> Likewise, ye wives, be in subjection to your own husbands; that, if any obey not the word, they also may without the word be won by the conversation of the wives; while they behold your chaste conversation coupled with fear. Whose adorning let it not be that outward adorning of plaiting the hair, and of wearing of gold, or of putting on of apparel; but let it be the hidden man of the heart, in that which is not corruptible, even the ornament of a meek and quiet spirit, which is in the sight of God of great price.

For after this manner in the old time the
holy women also, who trusted in God,
adorned themselves, being in subjection
unto their own husbands: **Even as Sarah
obeyed Abraham, calling him lord**:
whose daughters ye are, as long as ye do
well, and are not afraid with any amaze-
ment (1 Peter 3:1-6). (Emphasis added.)

God is concerned about a person's faith, character, integrity, and obedience to His Word, rather
than personality type. He is in the business of
conforming believers into the image of His Son
"that He might be the firstborn among many
brethren" (Romans 8:29). He has neither established personality categories in Scripture nor
identified people according to any temperament
typology. Nevertheless, Voges and Braund subject
numerous men and women of God to such an analysis and classification.

Just as LaHaye identified Abraham as a Phlegmatic, Voges and Braund make Abraham into a
High S (Steadiness) personality. In so doing, they
attempt to explain why he did what he did in terms
of the general traits assigned to that personality
type. They say:

Abraham is a marvelous example from
Scripture of a Steadiness personality style.
His life illustrates practical choices, team-
work, and always striving to be a peace-
maker. . . . To resolve the conflict, Abraham
was willing to allow Lot to choose where he

wished to settle and then go in the opposite direction.[8]

Thus, Abraham's actions are explained in terms of his inborn traits and personality type rather than in terms of his relationship to God.

But what about when Abraham led his men in pursuit of the kings who had defeated the kings of Sodom and Gomorrah and had kidnaped Lot? If one were to take that example, one might accuse Abraham of being High D (Dominant) instead of High S (Steadiness). According to Voges and Braund, a High S person avoids conflict. They say:

> Their need for security, peace, and support influences most High S people to place a tremendous importance on stability within their family. Should conflict exist among family members, they tend to become distressed and prone to worry and anxiety. This often leads to avoiding the conflict and letting others take the lead in creating solutions.[9]

Abraham certainly did not avoid the conflict or look to someone else to take the lead! Nevertheless, once someone has assigned a person to a category everything is interpreted in terms of that category. For instance, his trait of faithfulness and loyalty to his family took precedence over his so-called needs for security and peace. .

According to the temperament theories and personality profiles, all behavior can be understood, interpreted, and explained on the basis of temperament/personality. Anything a person does can be reduced to a person's basic temperament/personality type, because they see everything through that system.

Author and pastor Tommy Ice believes that imposing the DiSC system on various people in the Bible is a serious mistake in terms of interpreting Scripture. He says:

> Voges and Braund are imposing an external interpretative grid over the Bible which arrives at conclusions that various personalities of the Bible can be said to be illustrations of the DiSC system, thus giving the impression that this modern discovery of personality traits has always been there. I cannot see any difference, epistemologically, between using the DiSC grid as an interpretative framework for explaining the behavior of those in the Bible and that of the higher critical literary approaches of the Bible which produced things like the JEDP theory and two Isaiahs.[10]

In spite of their attempt to validate their typology with the Bible, Voges and Braund's book is simply a psychological tool which fits in well with the church's present infatuation with theories and therapies of counseling psychology. Their book's full title is revealing: *Understanding How Others Misunderstand You: A Unique and Proven Plan for Strengthening Personal Relationships*. The first part appeals to the currently popular psychological stance of victimhood. The reader is promised that by reading the book he will understand how **others** misunderstand him.

The subtitle presents the DiSC system as a "unique and proven plan." However, its uniqueness is lost in the plethora of systems that attempt to understand people by collecting a series of traits, distributing them among four categories and then putting people into the categories by matching traits and people. The only real element of uniqueness is a new vocabulary to identify old categories, and even that was adapted from Marston's DiSC model. Voges and Braund admit:

> The Greek words "Choleric," "Sanguine," "Phlegmatic," and "Melancholic" are synonymous terms to the DISC and used by some Christian writers to identify the differences in behavior. Most known is Dr. Tim LaHaye.[11]

Here's how the two systems line up:

LaHaye	**DiSC**
Choleric	Dominance
Sanguine	Influencing
Phlegmatic	Steadiness
Melancholy	Compliance[12]

Not only is Voges and Braund's version of DiSC not terribly unique; it is not proven from the perspective of scientifically established procedures with controls and strict research parameters. We say more about the *Personal Profile System* testing instrument in our chapter on personality tests and inventories.

In spite of exaggerated claims in their book title, Voges and Braund seem to be sincere people who evidently want to help people reach their greatest potential. They say:

> God desires for each person to realize his greatest potential. In Philippians 1:6 Paul writes "[I am] confident of this, that he who began a good work in you will carry it on to completion until the day of Christ Jesus." Understanding ourselves and others is a **prerequisite** for reaching our God-given potential.[13] (Emphasis added.)

The phrase "for each person to realize his greatest potential" is extensively used among godless humanists and pagan New Agers who emphasize human potential.

Any system that focuses on strengths and weaknesses of various temperament types is limited to reaching the greatest potential of what the Bible calls the "old man." In Philippians 1:6, Paul is **not** talking about people reaching their greatest potential through understanding themselves through temperament categories. He is talking about the Holy Spirit's work in each person through the process of sanctification whereby believers are transformed into the image of Christ.

As much as psychologists attempt to utilize the wisdom of man to improve the natural man or to enhance the sanctification process, the theories and therapies of the world are both intrinsically and ultimately at odds with the Word of God and the Work of the Holy Spirit. There is no biblical mandate to understand ourselves according to four categories of traits in order to reach a so-called "God-given potential." Great theological confusion arises when anyone attempts to mix godless systems of understanding the nature of man with what the Bible says about mankind and the dynamics of human behavior.

Loving Self.
Besides dispensing a questionable theory of personality based on personality types, Voges and Braund place an unbiblical emphasis on self. They attempt to support their unbiblical emphasis on self and self-love through misinterpreting such Scriptures as Matthew 22:39. Rather than presenting a biblically-sound exegesis, they misuse Jesus' words, "Love your neighbor as yourself," to support unbiblical doctrines of humanistic psychology. They say:

> Christ's second commandment, "Love your neighbor as yourself," is the cornerstone verse of this book. The only way we can ever love others in a self-sacrificial way is by first of all having a clear understanding of ourselves. That is because we must be

aware of how to take care of our own needs
(physical, emotional, and spiritual) before
we are capable of serving the needs of
others.

The Bible clearly supports the need for
developing love of ourselves and love of
others. You cannot have one without the
other. They go hand in hand. It is a
paradox, but you cannot serve in a self-
sacrificial way by sacrificing yourself. If
you sacrifice yourself without taking care of
your own needs, there is nothing of quality
left to give to others.[14]

Because humanistic self-love does not square with
Scripture, Voges and Braund call this a paradox.
But, it is not a paradox. It is a blatant contradiction
and reveals a clear disagreement between humanistic psychology and the Bible. Such a statement
really leaves God and His provisions out. We do not
love others because we love ourselves first. We love
others because God loved us first (1 John 4:19).

Their emphasis on loving and taking care of
self reflects the teachings of such secular humanists as Erich Fromm, who vehemently opposed
God's sovereignty and mocked Him as a self-seek-
ing authoritarian. Fromm taught that people must
love themselves to reach their highest potential. He
also taught that the source of love is within oneself.
That is why he believed that a person had to love
himself before he could love others. Without faith in
the love of God, a person is left in the bankruptcy of
self.

Voges and Braund attempt to justify self-love teachings that come from Fromm, Abraham Maslow, Carl Rogers, and others by saying, "The Bible clearly supports the need for developing love of ourselves and love of others."[15] But, there is no Scripture which supports "developing love for ourselves." That is why Christians who teach self-love resort to misunderstanding and misapplying Matthew 22:36-40. However, the concept of self-love is not the subject of the Great Commandment. "As thyself" is only a qualifier.

When Jesus was asked, "Master, which is the great commandment in the law?"

> Jesus said unto him, Thou shalt love the Lord thy God with all thy heart, and with all thy soul, and with all thy mind. This is the first and great commandment. And the second is like unto it, Thou shalt love thy neighbour as thyself. On these two commandments hang all the law and the prophets (Matthew 22:36-40).

In His answer, Jesus is not commanding people to love themselves. He does not give three commandments (love God, love neighbor, and love self). Instead, He says, "On these **two** commandments hang all the law and the prophets" (Matthew 22:40).

We are not commanded to love self. We already do. In fact, Jesus would not command people to love others as themselves unless they already **do** love themselves. It would be a pointless statement. If self-love were a necessity for loving others, it would have to precede love for God and love for others. To fit self-love theology, the first commandment would have to read: "Love yourself first so that you will be able to love God and others."

Scripture teaches that people already love themselves. Paul says, "For no man ever yet hated his own flesh; but nourisheth and cherisheth it, even as the Lord the church" (Ephesians 5:29). Biblical references to people loathing themselves have to do with knowing that their deeds are evil (e.g. Ezekiel 36:31). In those instances they are still committed to themselves and retain biases that are favorable to themselves until they turn to the Lord and confess their sin.

From the totality of Scripture, we are commanded to love others as much as we already love ourselves. The Good Samaritan story, which follows the commandment to love one's neighbor in the Gospel of Luke, illustrates not only who is our neighbor, but what is meant by the word *love*. Here love means to extend oneself beyond the point of convenience. The idea is that we should seek the good of others just as fully as we seek good for ourselves—just as we naturally tend to care for our own personal well-being. There is no hint that the Good Samaritan had to take care of his own needs first. That's what the priest and the Levite did. They took care of their own "needs" first. They loved themselves so that they could love others at their own convenience. Since it is natural for people to attend to their own needs and desires, Jesus turned their attention beyond themselves.

Biblical love for others comes **first** from God's love and then by responding in wholehearted love for Him (with all of one's heart, soul, mind and strength). A person cannot do that unless he knows Christ and is infused with His love and life. The Scripture says, "We love Him because He first loved us" (1 John 4:19). A person cannot truly love (*agapao*) God without first knowing His love by grace; one cannot truly love neighbor as self without first loving God. The proper biblical position for a Christian is not to encourage, justify, or establish self-love, but rather to devote one's life to loving God and loving neighbor as self. Dr. Jay Adams says:

> There is no need for concern about how to love one's self, for so long as one seeks first to love God and his neighbor in a biblical fashion, all proper self-concern will appear as a by-product. That is why the Bible never commands us to love ourselves. Since the Bible is silent on the matter, we should be too.[16]

Rather than teaching self-love as a virtue, the Bible lists self-love as one of the distinguishing marks of society during the last days:

> This know also, that in the last days perilous times shall come. For men shall be lovers of their own selves, covetous, boasters, proud, blasphemers, disobedient to parents, unthankful, unholy, without natu-

ral affection, trucebreakers, false accusers, incontinent, fierce, despisers of those that are good, traitors, heady, highminded, lovers of pleasures more than lovers of God; having a form of godliness, but denying the power thereof: from such turn away (2 Timothy 3:1-5).

The adjectives that describe "lovers of their own selves" certainly match up with the current increase in illicit entertainment, materialism, teenage rebellion, fornication, rape, adultery, divorce, drunkenness, hatred of God, and other forms of pleasure-seeking self-centeredness. Developing self-love is not the solution; it is a very large part of the problem.[17]

Need Psychology.
Along with self-love, Voges and Braund teach a number of other popular ideas related to need psychology. They say:

> This book is about understanding the basic differences in our needs-based behavior as opposed to differences in our values-based behavior. It focuses on the common differences in our behavior styles that relate to personality rather than to character.[18]

Such a distinction between needs and values is extrabiblical. Scripture does not distinguish between "needs-based behavior" and "values-based behavior."

The theory of emotional needs driving human behavior is not an important concept that must be added to the Bible. Nor must Scripture be assisted by such extrabiblical sources, because they are antithetical to God's Word. So-called needs-driven behavior is generally seen as non-moral. In Scripture behavior is understood in terms of obedience or disobedience to God. Either a person is pleasing God or not pleasing God. Even such mundane activities as eating are included. "Whether therefore ye eat, or drink, or whatsoever ye do, do all to the glory of God" (1 Corinthians. 10:31).

Along with their teachings on self-love and needs-driven behavior, Voges and Braund parrot the current vogue of codependency/recovery myths. They say:

> In a co-dependent relationship we become so absorbed in meeting someone else's needs that we can neither identify nor meet our own needs.[19]

Again, such a statement does not square with Scripture. There is no command for people to meet their own needs first so that they can meet the needs of others.

Voges and Braund are extending their influence into Christian churches, colleges and seminaries. They offer a secular system with a biblical facade, a simple device packaged in a scientific-looking format, and four updated labels by which to identify "behavioral styles." They use the exact same test and categories as in the secular instrument. Simply by interpreting biblical characters according to the *Classical Profile Patterns*, which is part of the *Personal Profile System*, they make their version "biblical" rather than secular.[20]

However, such systems present competing views of who man is and how he changes, and they corrupt the Scriptures with unproven, unscientific, and even paganistic philosophies of men. Unless a personality theory originates from studying Scripture and reflects sound biblical theology, it will tend to divert attention away from God and His Word concerning who man is and how he is saved and sanctified. Such deviation will present an alternate means of salvation and/or sanctification in addition to and in opposition to God's clear Word on the matter.

6

A Circus of Personality Types

The four temperaments and the DiSC are not the only shows in town. They may be the central ring attraction for their Christian enthusiasts, but there are other acts in the wings and sideshows.

P. T. Barnum believed that a good circus had "a little something for everybody."[1] And that's what's available in the wide array of personality typologies. There is a "little something" for everybody. To give you a glimpse of how many "little somethings" are available for personality typing, this chapter is devoted to looking at a few examples from the hundreds of personality typologies that appeal to the human desire to classify, categorize, and understand self and others.

Goody Two-Types.

"Two-four-six-eight; who do we appreciate?" And there are three's, nine's and sixteen's as well. Any number and any number of combinations will work for classifying temperaments and personalities. The two-types are simple ways of categorizing everyone. In spite of the great generality, it is amazing how many people think they can "really understand" a person once they put them into a category. Or, is it the other way around? They identify something about the person, think they've gained great insight into the other person and confidently shove them into a slot. We all do it. When was the last time you identified someone with one of the following two-dimensional personality classifications?

> Optimist/Pessimist
> Introvert/Extrovert
> Right Brain/Left Brain
> Cognitive/Emotional
> Loner/Joiner
> Type A/Type B

One writer, after examining a number of typologies came up with his own theory of types. He said:

> I propose that there are two kinds of people in the world: those who believe there are two kinds of people and those who don't. I place myself in the second category. How about you?[2]

Introversion/Extroversion.

Carl Jung's typology consists of the extroversion/introversion dichotomy with four basic psychic functions. Jung originally divided people into three groups: introverted, extroverted, and normal. He says of the normal group:

> . . . this group is the most numerous and includes the less differentiated normal man. . . . The normal man is, by definition, influenced as much from within as from without. He constitutes the extensive middle group, on one side of which are those whose motivations are determined mainly by the external object, and on the other, whose motivations are determined from within. I call the first group *extroverted*, and the second group *introverted*.[3]

It is interesting how Jung's abnormal categories have become household descriptives for everyone. How often have you heard someone referred to as an extrovert or an introvert? Is anyone "normal" these days?

Jung also distinguishes four basic psychic functions: sensation, thinking, feeling, intuition. From this he places people into corresponding groups:

> For complete orientation all four functions should contribute equally: thinking should facilitate cognition and judgment, feeling should tell us how and to what extent a thing is important or unimportant for us,

> sensation should convey concrete reality to
> us through seeing, hearing, tasting, etc.,
> and intuition should enable us to divine the
> hidden possibilities in the background,
> since these too belong to the complete pic-
> ture of a given situation.
>
> In reality, however, these basic functions
> are seldom or never uniformly differenti-
> ated.[4]

Therefore Jung divided people into four types:
sensation types, thinking types, feeling types, and
intuitives.[5] He then combined those types with
introversion and extroversion.[6]

Jung used such classifications in working with
neurotic individuals. He did not consider typing
normal people to be useful and even believed that
practice to be "a childish parlor game."[7] Nevertheless his system has been modified and popularized
by David Keirsey and Marilyn Bates in the book
*Please Understand Me: Character and Tempera-
ment Types*.[8] Keirsey and Bates present the same
system developed for the Myers-Briggs Type Indicator (MBTI).

Both the Keirsey-Bates typology and the MBTI
are based on the following pairs of opposite characteristics (polarities):

Extraversion (E)	vs	Introversion (I)
Intuition (N)	vs	Sensation (S)
Thinking (T)	vs	Feeling (F)
Judging (J)	vs	Perceiving (P)

When combined, there are sixteen types, which line up with various combinations of the four temperaments.[9] The book gives the same promises of understanding ourselves and others and of finding success in life as four temperaments books give.

Type A/Type B and Heart Disease.

Because the Greeks connected personality with bodily fluids, they connected personality with disease. People continue trying to make this kind of connection. Probably the most popular and well-known personality type related to disease is the "now-legendary" Type A.[10] The Type A person has been described and classified as being "aggressive, competitive, tense, time-conscious, hostile, and generally male."

For awhile it looked as if descriptive categories of Type A and Type B were going to be useful in identifying possible heart problems and preventing heart disease. Obviously the Type A's looked like the typical heart attack candidates. However, an article in *University of California, Berkeley Wellness Letter* says, "More than two decades of research into the relationship between personality and disease has found little significance." It further reports that a "22-year follow-up study of some 3,000 middle-aged men . . . indicated that Type A behavior was not related to heart attack deaths." The only personality trait they think might be related to heart disease is "chronic hostility or cynicism."[11]

A Cancer Personality?

Various researchers have attempted to connect diseases with personality types. One person came up with the following personality types: Heart-Disease Personality, High-Blood-Pressure Personality, and Cancer Personality. Descriptions of the Heart-Disease and High-Blood-Pressure types had more to do with body weight, eating, sleeping, smoking, and drinking than with personality characteristics. The Cancer Personality was described this way: "Little depression, anxiety, or anger, not close to parents, undemonstrative, ambivalence toward self and others."[12] Others contradict that description and identify the so-called Cancer Personality with depression. However, the current research does not support a disease-personality type of relationship.

An article in *The Johns Hopkins Medical Letter: Health After 50* reveals that there is no such thing as a "cancer personality." Numerous individuals have tried to connect depression with lowered immunity thus predisposing depressed people to getting cancer. Nevertheless that assumption has not been proved. A well-conducted longitudinal study of 6,403 men and women failed to show that depression was linked to cancer.[13]

Personality-Intelligence Types.

The triarchic theory, devised by Yale University professor Dr. Robert J. Sternberg, categorizes people on the basis of aspects of intelligence. The three types are described this way:

Componential type: "Alice had high test scores and was a whiz at test-taking and analytical thinking."

Experiential type: "Barbara didn't have the best test scores, but she was a superbly creative thinker who could combine disparate experiences in insightful ways."

Contextual type: "Celia was street-smart. She learned how to play the game and how to manipulate the environment. Her test scores weren't tops, but she could come out on top in almost any context."[14]

The advantage of Sternberg's system is that he at least takes into account more aspects of intelligence than the standard IQ tests and thereby encourages people to develop ways of making the most of what they have. His categories may also help some people to feel smarter than their test scores have shown. It is at least better than any kind of smart people/stupid people classification.

There is a fourfold classification system for managers that adds variables of Energetic and Lazy to Smart and Dull to designate four types of managers: Smart/Energetic, Smart/Lazy, Dull/Energetic, and Dull/Lazy.[15] Obviously one type looks lots better than the other types, but the others manage to keep on managing anyway. Perhaps the Dull/Lazy managers have Smart/Energetic workers to make up for the lack.

Four-Type Personality Classifications.

Many four-type personality systems are similar to the four temperaments but emphasize different aspects of personality. One strong promoter of the four temperaments has a list of other typologies that seem to fit major categories of the original four temperaments. As Solomon said, "There is no new thing under the sun" (Ecclesiastes 1:9). But there are nuances and alterations of old systems. Also, there is a multitude of ways of how one can categorize people by simply rearranging characteristics and emphasizing different aspects.

One classification of individuals promises to help you relate to people better simply by knowing if they are "Socializers," "Directors," "Thinkers," or "Relators." After listing the "primary needs" of each type, along with the "strengths" and "weaknesses," this typology promoter proceeds to tell his audience how to deal with each person.[16]

The idea is to "psych out" the person, tune into his wavelength, and punch the right keys to get him both to understand what you are saying and then to do what you want done. Sounds a bit manipulative. But, what if one makes an error categorizing the individual? What if he is a combination of types and the wrong balance of strategies is used? Never mind that. Just buy the program of cassettes, workbook and personal profile questionnaires and you'll be an expert. At least that's the implied promise.

Alternative (New Age) Types.

In his book, *Alternate Realities*, humanistic/ transpersonal psychologist Lawrence Leshan divides people into four categories by classifying them according to their view of reality. The four are "Sensory mode," "Clairvoyant mode," "Transpsychic mode," and "Mythic mode."[17] Believe it or not everyone fits these New-Age-sounding categories. But then the New Agers have to have a piece of the cake, too.

Psychologists have also designed personality types based on characteristics of various Greek gods and goddesses. Jungian analyst Jean Shinoda Bolen does more than classify people into personality types in her book *Goddesses in Everywoman*.[18] She classifies personality characteristics with goddesses (also referred to as archetypes) supposedly living in each woman. Women's personalities are then identified according to the dominance of one or more indwelling goddesses. Thus you have the Artemis woman, the Athena woman, and the Hestia woman, all with personalities reflective of the virgin goddesses. Then there are the "vulnerable" goddess-type women: the Hera woman and Persephone woman. And, finally the Aphrodite woman, dominated by the goddess of love and beauty.

Besides detailing each type and explaining how to handle one's particular dominant goddess or archetype, Bolen also gives examples of celebrities for each type. You can imagine her choices for the Aphrodite type of woman: Jean Harlow, Lana Turner, Marilyn Monroe, and Elizabeth Taylor.

Nancy Reagan is her example of a Hera woman.
Mother Teresa is the Hestia type. And she slaps the
Athena label on Phyllis Schlafly because one characteristic of the Athena woman in this mythological
typology is her tendency to defend patriarchal values and leadership.[19]

After her great success with the goddess types,
Bolen wrote *Gods in Everyman*.[20] Others have
expanded the horizon for men by giving them male
types and archetypes, such as King, Warrior,
Magician, and Lover.[21] Such typologies certainly fit
in with the New Agers' fascination with myths and
pagan worship.

One does not have to be a psychologist these
days to develop ways to classify people. A psychic
who "reads auras" wrote a book on how to classify
personality types by the colors of their supposed
auras. Even if one can't read auras, one can tell the
type and even the aura's color by reading each
type's characteristics.[22]

Four Types of Consumers.

A new typology for the marketplace is
"psychographics," a categorization based on "values
and lifestyles" related to buying. The shopper types
are color keyed according to whether they are
"outer directed," "inner directed," "need driven," or
"integrated." The "outer directed" type is the
largest group of consumers—a whopping 69 percent. Well, that should help the advertisers! Or
does it? Marketers use this typology to sell all kinds
of items, but results have been mixed.[23]

Animal Types.

What could be more endearing than animal types, especially if they are thought of as charming characters of Walt Disney fame? After their enchantment with the right brain/left brain pseudoscience, Gary Smalley and John Trent came up with a darling way to classify people. (Never mind that shamans identify with animals in their initiation rituals. Just keep Walt Disney in mind and enter Never-Never-Land.)

Using the Smalley/Trent "Personal Strengths Survey Chart," you can find out if you are a lion, beaver, otter, or golden retriever. You can take the test by circling various descriptions under L, B, O, or G and discover which animal you resemble most. A serious endeavor or harmless game? Just so no one takes it too seriously—or else we'll begin treating each other like animals.[24]

Smalley and Trent are not the only ones who have come up with a four-creature-type classification. Graphoanalyst Norman Werling, who supposedly discerns personality by analyzing handwriting, came up with butterfly, elephant, frog, and turtle types. Florence Littauer evidently considers Werling's typology of some value since she included it in her "Personality Comparison Chart," in which she lines up a number of other personality typologies with the four temperaments.[25]

An interesting reversal on animal types is the application of the four temperaments to dogs. Many of us remember Ivan Pavlov for conditioning dogs to salivate. Pavlov also noticed that dogs have different personalities. He categorized dogs into

four groups according to whether they had a
predominantly excitatory or predominantly inhibi-
tory nervous system or whether they were bal-
anced-steady or balanced-alternating as far as
being excited and inhibited. He then lined these up
with the four temperaments:

excitatory	choleric
inhibitory	melancholic
balanced-alternating	sanguine
balanced-steady	phlegmatic[26]

We can't leave this animal section without
mentioning the book *Dinosaur Brains: Dealing with
All Those Impossible People At Work.*[27] But since
the authors are really talking about the "reptilian
brain" in each of us, we'll skip this one and pick up
the pieces of the other broken-brain typologies in a
later section.

Physiological Models.

The four temperaments related to the four
bodily fluids are no longer accepted from a biological perspective, although in later centuries
other people developed different personality typologies based on individual biological make-up. For
instance, in the nineteenth century Léon Rostan
proposed a threefold typology and divided people
into digestive, muscular, and respiratory-cerebral
types. Then in the 1920s Ernst Kretschmer revived
Rostan's types and named them *pyknic, athletic,*
and *dysplastic.*[28] In the 1940s and 1950s William

Sheldon proposed three body types (somatotypes) and three temperament types and attempted to show correlations between the two.

Sheldon's three physical types were *endomorphy* (roundness with weight predominant near the digestive areas), *mesomorphy* (muscular build), and *ectomorphy* (long and slender). His three temperament types were *viserotonia* (loving comfort, food, and being with people), *somatotonia* (liking physical activity, power, and taking chances), and *cerebrotonia* (restrained, inhibited, and private). While at first glance one might assume that there is a correlation between the somatotypes and the temperament types, researchers have not been able to establish any relationship. Therefore, the somatotypes went out of vogue.[29]

Blood Type Personalities.

Just as the original four temperaments were based on some aspect of the body, numerous other typologies since then have also related the body to the personality. A few years ago a news article title was "Bloodtype reading new Japan rage; replaces astrology." The AP article from Tokyo said:

> The key to human behavior, once sought by Japan's amateur psychologists in the coursing of the stars, is now found by a new group of amateurs in people's bloodtypes.

Notice the universal characteristics for each blood type:

Type A	perfectionists
Type B	self-assertive, creative
Type AB	objective thinkers
Type O	discriminating, especially with
	friendships[30]

According to this system, all you need to know is someone's blood type and you can know whether to employ him and how to treat him if you do. Unfortunately for the enthusiastic users of this typology, the article also revealed, "Blood specialists and other experts call their theories groundless."[31] Nevertheless, at least one Christian gives it some credence, since she listed it in her "Personality Comparison Chart" and lined up the blood types with the four temperaments, of which she is extremely fond.[32]

Right-Brain/Left-Brain.

Personality types based upon alleged differences between right and left brain hemispheres have captivated the imagination of a number of people. Brain research that stimulated this typology had to do with brain-damaged persons. Initial findings were tentative and incomplete, and because they did not emphasize the interaction between the hemispheres of normal people, erroneous conclusions and speculations were made by people who were hearing about the research.

Those eager for new ways of categorizing people rushed in and created the so-called left-brained person (described as linear, logical, analytical, and unemotional) and the so-called right-brained person (described as spatial, creative, mystical, intuitive, and emotional).

Many people still believe in the right-brain/left-brain pseudoscience. Erroneously thinking the typology is supported by brain research, the right-brain/left-brain enthusiasts continue to embrace the initial implications, label them "science," and make all kinds of declarations about right-brain and left-brain people. Brain researchers are not happy about right-brain/left-brain personality typing, because it is misleading and misrepresents the vast complexity of the brain.

Neurologist Dr. John Mazziotta at the UCLA School of Medicine says:

> Even on the most trivial tasks our studies showed that everything in the brain was in flux—both sides, the front and back, the top and bottom. It was tremendously complicated. **To think that you could reduce this to a simple left-right dichotomy would be misleading and oversimplified.**[33] (Emphasis added.)

Biopsychologist Dr. Jerre Levy at the University of Chicago contends:

> **The two-brain myth was founded on an erroneous premise**: that since each hemisphere was specialized, each must function as an independent brain. But in fact, just the opposite is true. To the

extent that regions are differentiated in the brain, they must integrate their activities. Indeed, it is precisely that integration that gives rise to behavior and mental processes greater than and different from each region's contribution. **Thus, since the central premise of the mythmakers is wrong, so are all the inferences derived from it.**[34] (Emphasis added.)

After interviewing several researchers in the field, Kevin McKean says:

Scientists are understandably annoyed when they see careful but often inconclusive work popularized and exploited so glibly. As Deutsch puts it: "I get bothered by people saying, 'This is all based on neurological theory, therefore it's true.' It's not legitimized by neurological theory. **There is no evidence that people favor one portion of the brain or the other— that's pure speculation.**"[35] (Emphasis added.)

For more information about right-brain/left-brain typologies and their problems, see *Prophets of PsychoHeresy II.*[36]

Brain Quadrants.
Ned Herrmann piggybacked on the split-brain research, tied it in with the triune-brain theory of

Dr. Paul McLean, and came up with what he calls "preferred patterns of learning and knowing." He conceived of a system of four dominant types of learning and learners:

Cerebral left: rational, quantitative, technical,
> factual, intellectual.
> The dominant quadrant of many lawyers,
> engineers, bankers and doctors.

Limbic left: reliable, organized, conservative,
> detailed, "safekeeping."
> Popular among planners, administrators,
> bookkeepers and bureaucrats.

Limbic right: emotional, spiritual, helpful,
> personable, charitable.
> Nurses, musicians, social workers,
> teachers.

Cerebral right: open, risk-taking, visionary,
> fantasizing, impulsive.
> Entrepreneurs, artists, playwrights,
> trainers.[37]

Can you see yourself anywhere? Or are you factual, detailed, helpful, and open?

In spite of Herrmann's creative endeavor and his Brain Dominance Inventory,[38] there is no way to establish the validity of this typology without extensive observation of the brain's operation and the accompanying behavior of many individuals. His book, in which he presents this typology of personality and learning, costs $35, but to really know how to utilize his system one has to attend his workshops advertised at the end of his book.[39]

Color-Coded Thinking Types.

Also building on the two-brain model, Karl Albrecht combined abstract concepts and concrete experience with right-brain/left-brain and came up with Blue Sky (left-brained abstract), Red Sky (right-brained abstract), Blue Earth (left-brained concrete experience), and Red Earth (right-brained concrete experience).[40]

Sky represents abstract concepts and Earth represents concrete experience. Sounds vaguely like air (Sky), earth (Earth), fire (Red) and water (Blue) of Hippocrates' four humors. Albrecht connected blue with so-called left-brained analytical people and red with warm intuitive right-brained types. Thus he has a Red-Earth type ("intuitive, people-oriented and inclined toward direct experience") tending to "make decisions based on overall impressions rather than on individual facts or figures." He lined up sales, counseling, and social work with the Red-Earth type of person.[41]

Here is the promise Albrecht makes for his system:

> Did you know that your *thinking style* has a powerful influence on the way you relate to your world and to other people? The term "thinking style" refers to your own unique method of processing ideas and deriving meaning from your experience. Once you understand your thinking style, you can better appreciate the way other people communicate, make decisions, and solve their problems.[42] (Emphasis his.)

Notice there are four broad categories, but each person will find his "own **unique** method." What a pitch! You may think you understand yourself and others better, but all you've done is place them into a broad category, which may blind you to each person's uniqueness. Also remember, this system is based upon the split-brain personality myth and carries with it all the problems of the left-brain/right-brain nonsense.

Brain Chemical Types.

As you can tell by now, the brain is in vogue for classifying and typing people. Not only have people split the brain into sections and attributed personality characteristics accordingly, St. Louis psychiatrist Robert Cloninger has come up with one that connects three brain chemicals with behavior types. The brain chemical dopamine is connected with novelty seeking; the brain chemical serotonin with harm avoidance; and the brain chemical norepinephrine with reward dependence.

By combining the dominance of one or two of these brain chemicals, one can come up with various personality types.[43] For instance, he lists the following for a person high in novelty seeking (dopamine) but low in harm avoidance (serotonin):

> Danger Seeking
> Aggressive
> Competitive
> Overactive
> Impatient

Talkative

Extroverted[44]

But if a person is high in novelty seeking (dopamine) and also high in harm avoidance (serotonin) he is:

Hypothymic

Neurotic

Easily Distressed

Conflicted/Wavering

Uncertain/Indecisive[45]

Again, in spite of his elaborate descriptive charts and his use of personality questionnaires, Cloninger has not been able to establish his system's validity. Extensive recording of brain chemical levels along with objective observation of a large segment of the population would be necessary to validate this typology. While recent knowledge of brain chemicals makes the system appear more scientific than the four humors of Hippocrates, they are at about the same level of usefulness.

Future Fantasies (or Nightmares).

One of these days we will be able to put our blood type, body type, brain type, brain chemical type, hormone type, and maybe even our humor type all into a computer program and find out who we really are and to which personality group we belong. Instead of being assigned a number, we'll be given a personality type code. With all of the work on chromosomes, perhaps someone will come up with chromosome personality typing.

Possible categories might be Chromy W, Chromy X, Chromy Y, and Chromy Z. The possible combinations might be WXYZ or WWXZ or ZZZZ (extreme phlegmatic) or XXXX (extreme choleric). Then everyone can have a personality type code attached to his social security number and everyone will know how to relate to everyone else and we'll have peace on earth. You don't need to know my name anymore? You only need to know who I am? I'm 123-45-6789 Type WXYZ.

The Enneagram.

And last, but not least in the eyes of many who call themselves Christian, is the enneagram, which is an esoteric typology for self-understanding, personal growth, and transformation. Although it is purported to be an ancient spiritual tradition, it is relatively new to the Western world.

George Ivanovitch Gurdjieff, who brought the enneagram to Europe in the 1920s, claims it originated about 2500 years ago in a Babylonian wisdom school.[46] He taught that each person is born with a "planetary body type" with certain physical and psychological traits. He believed that a person's physical and psychological characteristics are related to a dominant endocrine gland and to planetary influences on that gland.[47] This may implicate the enneagram with Babylonian astrology, since those characteristics would be signified by a point on the enneagram. Gurdjieff's use of the enneagram also parallels the esoteric cabala's "Tree of Life" of Jewish mysticism.[48]

Gurdjieff used the esoteric elements of the enneagram with his students, but he did not formalize the system in written form. Therefore, others took this task upon themselves.

Oscar Ichazo began teaching the enneagram in Bolivia in the 1960s and brought his version of the nine personality types to the United States in 1971 as part of his Arica training. He claims to have learned the enneagram directly from Sufi teachers in Pamir before reading anything by Gurdjieff.[49] Ichazo's Arica training combines Eastern mysticism and Western psychology. The nine points on the circle's circumference are used to analyze ego types for gaining greater awareness and reaching a higher state of consciousness.[50]

Psychiatrist Claudio Naranjo learned Ichazo's system and taught the enneagram at Esalon, a human potential, New Age center in California. Among his students were several Jesuit priests who began to incorporate the enneagram into their counseling and into their own personal lives.[51] As a result, the enneagram's popularity has spread rapidly among Roman Catholics. In fact two of the most widely read books on the subject are written by a former Jesuit priest, Don Richard Riso.[52]

Although the geometric figure of the enneagram remains the same, versions of the enneagram personality typology differ among various teachers. Riso contends that his "interpretation of the enneagram . . . diverges from Ichazo's approach on a number of important points."[53] Helen Palmer's seminars and books also reveal a different emphasis and direction. In fact, her publisher says, "Ms Palmer has developed theories about the use of the enneagram in understanding human personality and its relationship to aspects of higher awareness that are different and distinct from those expounded by Mr. Ichazo."[54]

The enneagram is a geometric figure made up of a circle with nine points along the circumference, from which are drawn a triangle and an irregular hexagon. Each number represents one personality type and the lines indicate directions of integration and disintegration. The following chart gives the types according to Riso's and Palmer's type titles and according to Ichazo's personality "fixations":

	Riso	**Palmer**	**Ichazo**
1	Reformer	Perfectionist	Resentment
2	Helper	Giver	Flatterer
3	Status Seeker	Performer	Go
4	Artist	Tragic Romantic	Melancholy
5	Thinker	Observer	Stinge
6	Loyalist	Devil's Advocate	Coward
7	Generalist	Epicure	Planner
8	Leader	Boss	Venge
9	Peacemaker[55]	The Mediator[56]	Indolent[57]

Of course there are extensive descriptions of each type so that everyone can find himself and fit or squeeze into a type. Like other typologies, these are arbitrary categories.

The enneagram is as bad as the four temperaments for all of the same reasons. It has the same
problems with subjectivity, generality, trivializa-
tion of people, false assumptions and so on. It also
incorporates the same dangers. It is directly related
to the occult in its origins, its goals, and its present
use, including attempts to reach higher states of
consciousness. One enneagram critic says:

> Its occultic roots have not been thoroughly
> purged (if they can be), and it has opened
> itself to theological error and social and
> psychological misuse. The lack of scientific
> investigation means there are not controls
> to determine who actually is an expert, nor
> which advice is helpful or detrimental, nor
> whether the goals of the enneagram system
> are sound.[58]

The enneagram is another gospel. It is a path of
counterfeit salvation and should not be used by
Christians.

7

Typology Problems

Philosophical and psychological systems of the world seek to understand and explain the nature of man and how he is to live and change. But, they are human ways of trying to discover what God has already revealed through His Word. Unless such an investigation of the nature of man and why he is the way he is **originates** from the revealed Word of God, that investigation is going to be full of flaws and will either compete with or undermine Scripture and God's work in a person's life. That is what can easily happen when attempting to understand individual differences.

Observing and recording behavior objectively and accurately is difficult enough without involving presuppositions and subjectivity. When one goes beyond reporting observations and tries to explain the why's and how's, there is further danger of unbiblical presuppositions and contamination.

As fascinating as various personality types may be and as enticing as the four temperaments are, Christians must consider the serious implications of using such systems. Typologies are highly subjective contrivances that can lead to confusion, contradiction, superficiality, false assumptions and error. Furthermore, there are numerous spiritual reasons for not using temperament and personality typologies.

Objectivity and Subjectivity.

Some individual differences are more easily observed and measured than others, such as height, weight, and various external features. Others are impossible to quantify because of the subjectivity and influence of external circumstances. Describing, quantifying, measuring, and categorizing people according to temperament and personality all involve a high degree of subjectivity.

How does one measure even a single trait such as generosity apart from the circumstances in which a person has grown up and apart from the circumstances and people which might elicit generosity now? How does one measure optimism? Or, pessimism, enthusiasm, compassion, or friendliness? Or how does one measure revengeful, conservative, decisive, or independent?

While such descriptions may be applied more or less to people, how much is the more and how much is the less? And which traits are truly inborn (genetic), which are a combination of genes and environment, and which are mostly learned? Single trait dimensions are extremely difficult to quantify. Even more difficult are those attempts to categorize people accurately according to temperament or personality types.

Such type categories as the four temperaments are creations of fallen man. The categories are made up from human subjective observations of people, or they are revised from categories created by other fallen men. Various traits are then assigned to the categories, and all of this is contaminated by subjectivity. Then people are placed in the categories, again through subjectivity. Through further subjective observation or tests which rely on subjective responses, additional traits of people within the categories are observed. Thereby, the descriptions of the categories expand. Once categories are described, people assign themselves and others to them—again, through subjectivity. Even when research is used and tests are given, subjectivity reigns, both in test construction and in subjective responses.

Humans can only make subjective evaluations of themselves and others. Furthermore, such evaluations are often influenced by self-deception. Scripture is clear about this human tendency: "The heart is deceitful above all things, and desperately wicked: who can know it?" (Jeremiah 17:9). However, the Lord says: "I the Lord search the heart, I try the reins, even to give every man according to his ways, and according to the fruit of his doings" (Jeremiah 17:10).

Confusions and Contradictions.

While numerous typologies have been invented, there are some basic similarities among them. As with the temperaments, there is a grouping of descriptions and traits. There will also be polarities of traits between the types. And each type will have strengths and weaknesses. Nearly every system of grouping people according to temperament or personality types also allows combinations of types, since no one is able to fit into a pure type without some overlap. Each type is a gross generalization and a crude form of reference rather than a true description of any particular person.

On the other hand, various systems of typing people also reveal distinct differences among themselves. If one were to line up the various systems of typing people, there would be numerous inconsistencies. Even if one were to line them up according to certain generalities, there would still be enough differences to bring about confusion—if not contradiction.

Even though someone might think he has a very clear idea of each of the four temperaments, he will run into confusion when looking at various historical and current descriptions of those temperaments. For instance, early descriptions of the Melancholy were nearly always negative. As we noted earlier, some specific contradictions exist between the temperament chart of Dr. Hans Eysenck and that of Dr. Tim LaHaye. Both had to glean from historical sources to find their descriptions.

Superficiality and Error.

Most temperament or personality classifications oversimplify the complexity of individual differences. Such oversimplification leads to superficiality. Thus, temperament or personality type systems that are promoted as inside knowledge with special tools for understanding people actually lead to a more superficial knowledge of a person.

Such superficiality may lead to error, because the person is viewed according to the typology rather than according to his own unique characteristics. A review of personality types (including the four temperaments) in the *Encyclopedia of Psychology* says:

> The popularity of typologies can be understood in terms of the fact that they offer an economical way of summarizing complex configurations of variables—a way of characterizing the whole person in terms of a small number of very broad categories. The critics of typological description, on the other hand, have long contended that the simplicity of the typology leads to inaccuracy, that the typal categories are artificial, and that the distinctive features of the individual are lost when one is lumped together with many other people with distinctive qualities of their own.[1]

Watching movies and television gears people to personality typing because most characters are superficial types. They are rarely three-dimensional, fully developed characters. Showing that would be too tedious and take too long. Therefore, most acting parts are types and actors are often "type-cast." In a 30-minute, superficial thriller, the characters can be rather easily identified as types so there is a quick understanding of who's who. Even Shakespeare's characters were moderately portrayed within the four temperament types to make it easier for the audience to quickly identify the character and fill in the missing elements. But, if we view real people that way, we may know them only as intimately as sitcom characters. Real people are more than images on a screen. Real people are many-faceted. They should not be reduced to types. Once they are they become two-dimensional characters that may be very unlike who they really are. Viewing people through a temperament or personality type label depersonalizes the person and devalues his uniqueness.

Misplaced Assumptions.

If a person is put into one category because of certain seemingly consistent traits, there is often a misplaced assumption that other traits in that category apply when, in fact, they do not. For instance, if a person is identified as a Melancholy because he is quiet, reserved, and analytical, there may be unwarranted assumptions that he is also rigid, pessimistic, anxious, and moody.

In other words, if a few traits are identified as being representative of a temperament or personality type, then there are assumptions that he has other traits as well, even when he does not. Thus, people can develop extreme misunderstandings of one another when they use the temperament and personality typologies. When one or two traits are noticed, Bingo! The person is dropped into a slot that says he has numerous other traits that he may not have at all. Just because a person is calm and peaceful cannot give anyone the right to say he is a Phlegmatic and then say he must be lazy as well.

Typing people according to certain characteristics deceptively gives individuals a feeling that they know and understand another person. Such misplaced assumptions lead to relationships built on flimsy fabrications rather than on truth. Categories are often as artificial as comic book characters. They lead to superficial relationships and misunderstanding. They cause people to jump to conclusions and to exercise prejudice—not based on race but on personality type. Furthermore, using typologies may be a way to say, "I don't want to take the time to discover who you really are."

Generalities May Appear to be Specifics.

Typology systems are especially appealing to people who are willing to take gross generalities and broad categories and apply them uniquely to themselves and others. The wonderfully captivating aspect of personality-type systems like the four temperaments is their easy applicability to all people. Since there are enough general descriptive elements for every category, everyone is sure to fit somewhere. And because every system of personality classification allows for combinations of types, no one is left out.

Virtually everyone can be placed somewhere in some combination of types, because each category is filled with general, universal descriptions of people. Descriptive characteristics of particular categories, such as "quiet and thoughtful," may not be as distinguishing as one might think. Is there anyone who has never been quiet and thoughtful? Such personality typologies are thus based upon gross generalities and people are placed in broad categories that can only lead to superficial knowledge and understanding of anyone. Unfortunately, however, most people accept such character descriptions as uniquely applicable to themselves and others. This is called the "Barnum Effect."

False Assumptions about Consistency.

Those who use typologies often seem to assume that characteristics are consistent within a variety of circumstances. Nevertheless, people act in various ways in varying circumstances. For instance, in the family constellation or around good friends a person may be very outgoing and sociable, but be quiet and reserved in different circumstances, in unfamiliar surroundings, or among strangers. In *Personality and Assessment*, Walter Mischel says that "with the possible exception of intelligence, highly generalized behavioral consistencies have not been demonstrated, and the concept of personality traits as broad response predispositions is thus untenable."[2]

Spiritual Reasons for Not Using Typologies.

Besides all of the above problems with using temperament or personality types, there are spiritual reasons why the four temperaments and similar typologies are dangerous for Christians. The four temperaments and similar typologies give false power based upon a lie. The Word of God is true. It is quick and powerful. To replace or assist it with erroneous personality typologies is an insult to the Lord, especially considering the occult relationship.

Spiritual dangers of using temperaments and personality typologies can be seen in the following activities:

1. Evaluating the nonphysical aspects of a person (soul/spirit) according to an extrabiblical model.

2. Dividing people into categories that emphasize the flesh rather than the spirit.

3. Replacing sanctification with self-improvement through strengthening the positive aspects of the temperament.

4. Focusing on self-identity according to temperament rather than our new identity in Christ.

5. Becoming self-focused and minding the things of the flesh.

6. Excusing sinful behavior.

7. Walking according to the temperament theory instead of walking after the Spirit.

8. Attempting to become righteous through works: enhancing strengths and overcoming weaknesses. (Positive temperament traits cannot be equated with the fruit of the Spirit. They come from the wrong source.)

9. Being drawn away from dependence on Christ to dependence on a system.

10. Receiving false power based upon a lie.

11. Viewing one another according to the philosophies of men, according to the elementary principles (the four elements, the four temperaments).

12. Disregarding Paul's warning applies to the use of the four temperaments:

> Beware lest any man spoil you through philosophy and vain deceit, after the tradition of men, after the rudiments of the world, and not after Christ (Colossians 2:8).

Throughout the Bible God warns His people about the dangers of following the ways of the surrounding nations. Yet, over and over again His people turned to idolatry and other occult practices forbidden by God. We are in grave danger of repeating Israel's sins by following after the world's ways and even by entering into the deception of occult wisdom and practices.

The practice of astrology is not simply limited to knowing various charts and relating the configurations of the sky with the person's birth. Astrologers have admitted they receive psychic knowledge about people beyond their abilities to use and understand the horoscope. They are evidently given special information concerning individuals through demons. Similarly, anyone who reads auras and types people accordingly receives information from demon spirits.

To the degree that the four temperaments are related to astrology is the possibility for similar occult, psychic activity. Wherever there is deception, place is given to the devil. He may appear as an angel of light and even give uncanny insight into people. Because of that possibility, Christians who have been depending on the four temperaments and related typologies to understand their spouses and children would be wise to confess their involvement with this ungodly system, repudiate it in the name of Jesus, and flee from further contamination.

8

Psychological Testing

Psychological testing is essentially a twentieth-century phenomenon. With the rise of science and the use of mathematics in the nineteenth century, hope was raised that mathematical models could be harnessed to understand and explain man and to make predictions about him. The hope is that, through the use of mathematics, psychological tests can be developed that will use a small sample of man's behavior (as exhibited on the test) to reveal a great deal more about him.

In her book *Psychological Testing*, Dr. Anne Anastasi gives a general definition of a psychological test. She says:

> A psychological test is essentially an objective and standardized measure of a sample of behavior.[1]

The test is an attempt to diagnose some broad and significant aspect of an individual's behavior in order to reveal something about him or to predict how he will perform in the future. Anastasi says:

> Traditionally, the function of psychological tests has been to measure differences between individuals or between reactions of the same individual on different occasions.[2]

Numerous tests and types of tests have been developed to measure these differences. Psychological tests can be categorized under the following three general headings: 1) tests of general intellectual level, 2) tests of separate abilities, and 3) personality tests. Our primary concern is with the last category, which includes personality inventories and temperament tests. However, before we go into detail, it is necessary to introduce two psychological testing features which are extremely important: reliability and validity.

Every psychological test has numerous important features of construction and use. We will only describe two of them: reliability and validity. As we discuss those two terms in particular and later apply them to personality testing specifically, we will simplify as much as possible. Our goal in this chapter is to make this complex subject as clear as possible to help the reader understand the issues presented in the next chapter.

The first term, *reliability*, refers to consistency. Anastasi says:

Test reliability is the consistency of scores
obtained by the same persons when
retested with the identical test or with an
equivalent form of the test.[3]

For example, if an individual takes an IQ test on
Monday and Friday of the same week and receives
IQ scores of 90 and 91 respectively, it is obvious
that there is consistency between the two scores
and that some confidence may be placed in the
results.

If test/retest consistency happens often enough,
with enough individuals, we will gain more and
more confidence in the test's reliability. However, if
an individual takes an IQ test on Monday and
Friday of the same week and scores 90 and 120
respectively, the inconsistency of scores indicates a
lack of reliability and no confidence can be taken in
either score. The more often test/retest inconsistency occurs the less confidence one can take in the
reliability of the test.

The minimum requirement for a test is that it
must demonstrate reliability over time. However,
reliability alone is not enough. Even if a test is
highly reliable (consistent) it may still lack meaning. In other words, it may be consistent, but it may
be consistently wrong. That is why the term
reliable may be a bit misleading. A test that is
reliable in terms of consistency may not be reliable
in terms of accuracy or in terms of giving the
information it is designed to give. For example, an
individual may score at or near 90 on several
administrations of an intelligence test, but really be
far more intelligent by other measures.

In addition to being reliable, a test result must also be valid. Anastasi says: "The validity of a test concerns *what* the test measures and *how well* it does so."[4] (Emphasis hers.) She also says: "Undoubtedly the most important question to be asked about any psychological test concerns its validity."[5]

While reliability means consistency of test results, validity can be thought of as the integrity of the test results. While reliability can be measured by comparing repeated results by the same individual on the same test (or an equivalent form), validity is best measured by comparing the test result with an independent, objective standard. We offer the following example to clarify these two concepts.

Let's say an individual takes a computer typing test one day a week for three consecutive weeks and each time scores approximately 30 words per minute. The reliability is excellent thus far. Let's say that he takes the same test for three more weeks and scores about 30 words per minute each time. The reliability is better yet. If we add more individuals with similarly consistent results based upon various individual typing speeds, we are led to greater and greater confidence in the test's reliability. However, we said earlier that a test could be reliably wrong.

While reliability is important, validity is far more important. Lack of validity on a test would demonstrate that even though that particular test may be reliable, it should not be trusted.

Validity, at its best, involves some external, objective standard against which to compare test results. If, in the typing test example, we had an external, objective standard against which to measure, we could then judge the test results. What if the typist who consistently scored 30 words per minute on the typing test also typed at a computer at work? And, what if the computer had a software package that measured his typing speed and that software consistently showed that he generally typed approximately 60 words per minute? The typing test would be reliable for this individual, but not valid because of the great discrepancy between the typing test results and the external results from his software package at work. Likewise if a substantial discrepancy existed for a large group of individuals, then the use of the test would be questionable.

In the next two chapters we will be dealing with this most important characteristic of validity, which is most ideally obtained by comparing results on the same test (or an equivalent form) with an external, objective criterion. We will be looking for this most important characteristic of validity as we examine personality inventories and temperament tests.

9

Personality Testing

Personality tests "are instruments for the measurement of emotional, motivational, interpersonal, and attitudinal characteristics, as distinguished from abilities."[1] While there is a variety of personality tests, we will be focusing our attention on personality inventories. These inventories are known as self-report inventories. They are structured so that the test taker is forced to make choices that best describe himself.

Some tests provide statements to which the test taker merely responds "True" or "False." Other tests provide statements to which an individual responds with "most like me" or "least like me." Others force the test taker to choose one among several descriptive words or phrases. These are but three examples of the various forced choices a test taker is provided.

Probably the most popular of the personality inventories used in the church are the Myers-Briggs Type Indicator (MBTI), the Personal Profile System (PPS), and the Taylor-Johnson Temperament Analysis (TJTA). We will discuss each test including the issue of its validity (integrity). Also, we will discuss some other instruments that claim to measure temperament and spiritual gifts.

As mentioned earlier, validity is "the most important question to be asked about any psychological test."[2] Another way to think about validity is to imagine that one attempts to validate a drug used to cure an illness. If the drug is purported to cure an illness and is scientifically tested and found lacking, one would certainly not use the drug or recommend it to others. A drug that has not proven itself would not even be on the market. If it were, there would be a public outcry against it and the Federal Drug Administration (FDA) would ban its sale.

However, because there are no such agencies or regulations curbing the use of psychological tests and because tests are not foreign substances ingested to cure illness, many psychological tests continue to be used in spite of their lack of validity. A good example of this is the Rorschach inkblot test, which is a projective technique.

The Rorschach inkblot test was developed by Swiss psychiatrist Hermann Rorschach and has been used for more than 60 years. The test consists of 10 cards. Each card has a bilaterally symmetrical inkblot on it. Five cards are black and white and the other five are colored. An examiner shows the cards to the individual and asks him to describe what he sees. The examiner evaluates the person's responses according to specified guidelines.

The guidelines reveal the test's religious bias. If a person sees religious symbols, those responses will generally be scored as abnormal. The *Rorschach Interpretation: Advanced Technique* authors say:

> Religion contents are virtually never present in the records of normals. Their occurrence is associated with profound concern about the problems of good and evil, concern which, almost always, is a screen for and displacement of guilt induced by sexual preoccupation. Religion contents may be used to infer critical and unresolved problems of sexuality . . . [religion] responses are most common among schizophrenics, particularly patients with delusions which concern religion.[3]

One wonders how many unsuspecting Christians might have taken the Rorschach and consequently been treated for sexual preoccupation.

Everyone seems to know about this seemingly magical instrument, but few lay people question its validity. At least one million people took the test each year during the mid-sixties. About five million hours of administering and scoring added up to a whopping $25,000,000 per year.[4] Although there has been a slight decline, the Rorschach has continued to be used at a rate of nearly a million per year which would equal a much larger bill at today's prices.[5]

Even though psychotherapists are aware of studies that reveal the Rorschach's poor validity, they continue to use it. Why? Because they hope to discover at least one hidden clue to understanding the person. Yet, what do they really find? Hidden treasure? Or is the treasure they are looking for as elusive as the pot of gold at the end of the rainbow? In purporting to reveal and even measure the personality's deepest levels, the Rorschach cannot even help anyone distinguish between fool's gold and the real thing.

After an extensive analysis of the Rorschach inkblot test and review of the literature, Arthur Jensen presents his conclusion in the *Mental Measurements Yearbook*. He says:

> Put frankly, the consensus of qualified judgment is that the Rorschach is a very poor test and has no practical worth for any of the purposes for which it is recommended by its devotees.[6]

Anastasi says:

> The accumulation of published studies that have *failed* to demonstrate any validity for such projective techniques as the Rorschach . . . is truly impressive.[7] (Emphasis hers.)

The Rorschach and other personality tests of poor validity have been used far too long. Yet, it will be even longer before they are abandoned. As long as horoscopes remain in vogue, the Rorschach and other personality tests will also retain their mystique.

All psychological tests have problems, but personality inventories are even more problematic. Anastasi says, "The construction and use of personality inventories are beset with special difficulties over and above the common problems encountered in all psychological testing."[8] This remark can just as easily be applied to temperament tests. The difficulties involved in personality inventories, profiles and tests could fill up a book in themselves. However, we will restrict ourselves to the issue of validity.

Validity.

One author of *The Myth of Measurability* says, "Validity is the soul of a test." He goes on to say, "It is here that most discussions of testing run aground and most informed proponents of tests fall silent."[9] Industries and businesses often use personality tests to find out if a prospective employee's personality is suited to a particular job description. The idea is to predict the subsequent success of that particular applicant.

In spite of most people believing that such tests really do what people think they do, a *Training* magazine article reports that "the most extensive surveys done on these instruments [personality tests] over the years have shown their prediction power to be exceedingly weak." An individual who conducted one such study said, "One cannot survey the literature on the use of personality tests in industry without becoming thoroughly disenchanted."[10]

When we introduced the concept of validity we said that the validity of a test indicates its integrity, whether it actually measures what it is supposed to measure and how well it does so. One might assume there is just one kind of validity, one kind of objective means of determining if the test does what it claims to do. However, there are several ways to determine validity.

Validity is generally grouped under three principal categories: 1) content-related validity, 2) criterion-related validity, and 3) construct-related validity. A brief discussion of each may be helpful to understand problems intrinsic to personality inventories and other such tools used to analyze temperaments and traits.

Content-related Validity.

Content-related validity works very well in education. For example, we write a test to measure what students learned in math. The test is valid to the extent that we ask questions about math and not football. One can see clearly item by item whether the questions are about math and not some other field of study.

One might claim content-related validity for personality inventories and temperament tests, since the items seem to have appropriate content.

"Do you like to perform on stage?" seems to have the right content for extroversion, for instance.

However, one problem with content-related validity as applied to personality inventories and similar tests is circularity. The test measures extroversion because it defines extroversion by the questions it asks. Conversely, in a test of accumulated knowledge the content has been taught before the test is given. For instance, in giving a math test we would have covered the math content before the math test was given, rather than define the content (extroversion) by the test ("Do you like to perform on stage?") In other words, the answers on a math test do not define the content.

Because of such circularity and other problems, Anastasi says that for personality tests "content validation is usually inappropriate and may, in fact, be misleading." She contends that the content of personality tests "can do little more than reveal the hypotheses that led the test constructor to choose a certain type of content for measuring a specified trait. Such hypotheses need to be empirically confirmed to establish the validity of the test."[11]

Test takers are often fooled because the content seems to be about what the test purports to measure, such as extroversion. But, this does not establish the validity of such tests. Also, many who read books by individuals such as LaHaye, Littauer, Voges and Braund are fooled into believing in the content of their teachings because they are unaware of the necessity for validity.

Criterion-Related Validity.

Another form of validity is criterion-related validity. Anastasi says:

> Criterion-related validation procedures indicate the effectiveness of a test in predicting an individual's performance in specified activities. For this purpose, performance on the test is checked against a *criterion*, that is, a direct and independent measure of that which the test is designed to predict.[12]

Two areas of criterion-related validity on temperament and personality tests can be brought out by asking two questions:

1. What is Mary like? (Diagnosis)
2. Can we predict how Mary will do as a result of this instrument? (Prediction)

The first question has to do with whether Mary really has a particular temperament or personality profile. It is a question of whether she has been diagnosed accurately. The second question asks if the instrument (test or inventory) will enable us to predict how Mary will act and whether she will succeed or fail in the future as a result of having a particular temperament or personality.

We do not wish to get into the complexities of criterion-related validity as it pertains to personality inventories and tests. We bring it up because so many personality profiles and temperament tests are offered and appraisals made that are wholly without statistical validation. As you read various popular books, take various popular personality inventories and temperament tests, and hear about being able to predict future behavior as a result, remember that criterion-related validity (diagnosis and prediction) is a must before you accept the results with confidence. If a test has not been validated, do not bother with it. Requiring criterion-related validity would probably eliminate all of the known temperament tests and many of the personality inventories.

Construct-Related Validity.

The third type of validity is construct-related validity. According to Anastasi, "The construct-related validity of a test is the extent to which the test may be said to measure a theoretical construct or trait."[13] In our earlier example of a typing test there was an external exact measure of typing speed which occurred at the individual's work station. It was then possible to validate the individual's test station results. However, in personality testing, the constructs are hypothetical or conceptual. You can't easily quantify personality traits or temperament types. Unlike the typing test, in which the quantities of 30 wpm and 60 wpm were exact measuring units, the traits and types are not. It is necessary in these instances to infer validity through a very sophisticated statistical process, which has obviously not been done in too many instances.

Transparency of Test Items.
There are numerous reasons for lack of validity
on personality tests. One major reason why there
are problems with validity is the transparency of
the test items. Anastasi says:

> Self-report inventories are especially sub-
> ject to malingering and faking. Despite
> introductory statements to the contrary,
> most items on such inventories have one
> answer that is recognizable as socially
> more desirable or acceptable than the
> others.[14]

Because of this, individuals are able to "fake good"
to give a good impression and "fake bad" to create a
bad impression. There is plenty of evidence of this
in the research literature even to the extent that
when the same person takes the same test twice he
can produce two different results as he wills.[15]
Martin Gross, in his book *The Brain Watchers*,
gives an excellent example of faking. He describes
how he helped a friend prepare for a test to apply
for a position in a large corporation:

> The night before his encounter, we sat reso-
> lutely at his dining room table preparing
> for the grand experiment. The major test
> was the Edwards Personal Preference, a
> forced-choice test specifically designed to
> thwart such perverse attempts at image
> building.[16]

First Gross had his friend take the test without any coaching. He says:

> The result was grizzly: a friendly (very high "nurturance"), lively (high "change"), self-thinking (high "autonomy") individual with absolutely no desire to manipulate the puppet strings of destiny (low "dominance" or "leadership").[17]

It was obvious to Gross that his friend would not get the job with that kind of profile. Therefore, the two of them tried to imagine what the corporation was looking for. They came up with a list of traits he would have to score high on and those that he should keep pretty well near average. They then went through the test item by item "until we had *exactly* duplicated our estimate of the corporate ideal."[18] (Emphasis his.) The next morning the individual took the test. He was hired with the compliment that his test results were "exceptional." Not only were his test results exceptional; so was his performance on the job![19]

If Not Validity, Then What?

Personality and temperament tests and inventories generally have extremely poor validity. In other words they cannot be trusted to do what they are created to do. In spite of the great confidence so many people have in such tests for personal understanding and corporate hiring, such tests just have not met the rigors of validity.

As an example of the untrustworthiness of such tests, Gross decided to try a little experiment. This time he himself took a battery of tests as carefully and as honestly as he could to see if the results would be consistent. After scoring and comparing the results he says:

> When digested, with consummate professional "caution," what could it all tally? Obviously, an extroverted hermit, both morose and happy, an unemployable who responds beautifully to corporate life, the average pedestrian soul who stands head-to-ego above the crowd, in a spectacularly adjusted, but highly neurotic way.[20]

While such an anecdote may be humorous, the possibility of erroneous scores and inaccurate profiles is not at all funny. There are serious consequences when truth is violated with tests that appear to be as trustworthy and as objective as a perfect mathematical equation, but miss the mark. Based upon academic information alone, it is our opinion that if the personality inventories and temperament tests were labeled as drugs, the Federal Drug Administration would ban their sale and use.

10

Popular
Personality Tests

There are numerous personality tests having to do with types, temperaments, traits, interests, values, attitudes, and even spiritual gifts. Some tests are quick and casual; others are complex and detailed. Some are interest inventories designed to assist in career choices and employment. Others are designed for self-knowledge. In this chapter we will discuss a few of the tests that are extensively used by Christians.

Myers-Briggs Type Indicator (MBTI).
The Myers-Briggs Type Indicator (MBTI) is a personality inventory based on Carl Jung's theory of psychological types. The MBTI provides the following four bipolar scales:

Introversion—Extroversion
Sensing—Intuition
Thinking—Feeling
Judging—Perceiving

These four scales yield 16 possible types.

The National Research Council has evaluated the MBTI. The Council members are drawn from the councils of the National Academy of Sciences, National Academy of Engineering, and Institute of Medicine. In appraising the MBTI, the National Research Council says:

> McCaulley (1988) estimates that the MBTI is used as a diagnostic instrument by 1,700,000 people a year in the United States, and Moore and Woods (1987) list the wide variety of organizations in business, industry, education, government, and the military that use it. It is probably fair to say that the MBTI is the most popular "self-insight, insight into others" instrument in use today. Unfortunately, however, the popularity of the instrument is not coincident with supportive research results.[1]

In other words, research results do not support the popularity! The Council's particular concern is the lack of validity for the MBTI. In concluding the section on validity the Council states: "The evidence summarized in this section raises questions about the validity of the MBTI."[2]

The Council also criticizes the marketing of the MBTI:

> From the perspective of the instrument's developers, the profits from an audience eager for self-improvement encourages them to market the instrument aggressively; aggressive marketing—complete with type coffee mugs, t-shirts, pins, license plates—has apparently increased the number of consumers worldwide.[3]

Prior to their overall "Conclusions" section, the Council says that "the popularity of this instrument in the absence of proven scientific worth is troublesome." In their "Conclusions" section, the Council says very clearly: "At this time, there is not sufficient, well-designed research to justify the use of the MBTI in career counseling programs."[4]

Others have expressed concern about the difficulty of establishing validity for tests that are based upon a theoretical construct. Drs. L. J. Cronbach and P. E. Meehl say:

> Unless substantially the same nomological net is accepted by the several users of the construct public validation is impossible. A consumer of the test who rejects the author's theory cannot accept the author's validation.[5]

In applying this idea to the MBTI, Dr. Jerry Wiggins says:

The validity of the MBTI can be evaluated independently of the total corpus of Jung's writings but it cannot be fairly appraised outside the more delimited context of Jung's theory of psychological types. As with any construct-oriented test, both the validity of the test and the validity of the theory are at issue.[6]

Please note that the validity of the test and the validity of the theory are inextricably bound.

Carl Jung viewed all religions as collective mythologies, not real in essence, but real in their effect on the human personality. For Jung, religion, though merely a myth, was an indispensable spiritual support.[7] Jung was quite familiar with Christianity. His father was a minister. Describing his experience with Christianity he says:

Slowly I came to understand that this communion had been a fatal experience for me. It had proved hollow; more than that, it had proved to be a total loss. I knew that I would never again be able to participate in this ceremony. "Why, that is not religion at all," I thought. "It is the absence of God; the church is a place I should not go to. It is not life which is there, but death."[8]

Jung's essential misunderstanding of Christianity, the Church, and Holy Communion carried over into his psychological theories.

From his rejection of Christianity Jung could have proceeded to deny all religions. Instead, he chose to see them all as myths, as symbolic expressions of the inner psyche. He combined this interest in religion as myth with his practice of psychoanalysis to such a degree that Viktor Von Weizsaecker declared, "C. G. Jung was the first to understand that psychoanalysis belonged in the sphere of religion."[9] Because psychoanalysis was a form of religion for Jung, he could not reject all religion without rejecting psychoanalysis itself. In presenting all religion as mythology and fantasy, Jung debased the spirituality of man and defied the God of the Bible.

Rather than believing the Bible and following the Holy Spirit, Jung followed his own spirit guide. In *Memories, Dreams and Reflections*, Jung says:

> Philemon and other figures of my fantasies brought home to me the crucial insight that there are things in the psyche which I do not produce, but which produce themselves and have their own life. Philemon represented a force which was not myself. In my fantasies I held conversations with him and he said things which I had not consciously thought. For I observed clearly that it was he who spoke, not I.[10]

Jung's theories were developed while under the influence of his spirit guide.

Theories that underlie personality inventories, temperament tests, and spiritual gifts inventories are not science. We have dealt with this subject in detail elsewhere and shown that such theories are merely the opinions of men.[11] For example, Jung's fourfold preferences are his opinion about man. The use of them in a personality test such as the MBTI is Jung's theory (which is just his opinion, not science) put in test form. Every personality inventory or temperament test depends upon someone's personal opinion.

Just because someone devises a test and uses the four Jungian personality preferences (and 16 types) and uses mathematical means of validating it does not mean that the theory behind it is scientific or factual. For example, one could create a personality inventory based upon Freud's four psychosexual stages of development. The four stages are oral, anal, phallic, and genital.

One could then set up a system of four preferences and 16 types based upon the Freudian system in the form of a personality inventory. With much psychometric work, one could eventually create a test with reliability and validity results at least equal to that of some current tests. However, if the underlying theories are not scientific and especially if they originated from the occult, why would one care about reliability or even validity?

At minimum, Jung's theory is merely vain philosophies of men against which we are warned in Scripture. At worst, it originated from Satan through a spirit guide. We would think that no Christian would want Jung's psychological theory or any test that derives from it.

We interviewed a woman who is an Association for Psychological Types (APT) member. She speaks at their conferences and is very familiar with the MBTI, having used and taught it for years. We asked her if there was a relationship between the MBTI and the four temperaments. She said there definitely was and that this is often the topic at APT conferences.

The relationship between Jung's psychological types and the four temperaments can best be seen in the book *Please Understand Me: Character and Temperament Types* by David Keirsey and Marilyn Bates. Keirsey and Bates discuss the four temperaments, but choose to use the names of four Greek gods "whom Zeus commissioned to make man more like gods."[12] The gods they have selected to represent the four temperament types are Apollo, Dionysus, Prometheus, and Epimetheus. Keirsey and Bates discuss the Apollonian Temperament, the Dionysian Temperament, the Promethean Temperament, and the Epimethean Temperament.

The MBTI, because of its involvement in the four temperaments, even though in a Jungian form, is subject to the same criticisms that we directed earlier at those who directly use the four temperaments. Christians should not administer or take the MBTI. For both biblical and scientific reasons, the MBTI should not be used to evaluate individuals for Christian service or for personal understanding.

Personal Profile System (PPS) and
Biblical Personal Profiles (BPP).

Like the MBTI, the Personal Profile System is a personality inventory based on Carl Jung's theory of psychological types. However, in addition to Jung's theory, the PPS is based upon a book by William Marston, *Emotions of Normal People*. The PPS provides the following four scales:

> D — dominance
> i — influencing of others
> S — steadiness
> C — compliance (to their standards)[13]

To better understand the PPS, we obtained copies of it and of the Biblical Personal Profiles (BPP). The 24 groups of words used on both tests are identical. Therefore our comments about the PPS apply equally to the BPP. After reading the two tests and all the other materials we received from Performax Systems International, Inc., we looked at the academic sources for evaluations and reviews. We found very few references in the academic literature for the PPS and none for the BPP.

In the Performax Product Catalog is a listing for *The Kaplan Report: A Study of the Validity of the Personal Profile System*. We obtained a copy of that report. It says:

> Since 1972 the PPS has been widely employed. The market for this product is said to be growing daily. Hence, in 1982,

> PSII [Performax Systems International, Inc.] contracted with Kaplan Associates of Chevy Chase, Maryland for the conduct of a study to establish how the PPS compares as an assessment instrument with highly researched and valid psychological measuring instruments.[14]

Please notice that Performax, the company that owns and markets the PPS, contracted with a firm, Kaplan Associates, to conduct this study. We have read the report and have concerns and questions about it. It definitely does not establish the necessary validity for the PPS.

One of the most important volumes on tests is the *Mental Measurements Yearbook* (MMY). There is no mention of the PPS in the MMY until *The Tenth Mental Measurements Yearbook*. In that volume, the PPS is evaluated. This recent evaluation occurred years after *The Kaplan Report*. We quote from that review:

> A serious concern with this instrument is its lack of reported research. While the authors state the instrument shows good reliability and validity, they provide the user with virtually no data to support these claims.[15]

The reviewer goes on to refer to and then challenge studies that are provided in the PPS manual. In conclusion, the reviewer says that **"the clear lack of data to support this instrument should**

preclude its use."[16] (Emphasis added.) We did a
literature search on the PPS and found other
reviews that substantiated the MMY recommendation.

Because the PPS and the BPP are related to
Jungian theory, the same remarks made in the
MBTI section would apply. These are not tests that
Christians should be involved in or promote. The
PPS and the BPP are also quite frank about the
relationship of the DiSC and the four tempera-
ments. As we quoted earlier, its test material says:

> "The Greek words "Choleric," "Sanguine,"
> "Phlegmatic," and "Melancholic" are synon-
> ymous terms to the DISC and used by some
> Christian writers to identify the differences
> in behavior. Most known is Dr. Tim
> LaHaye.[17]

As mentioned earlier, the PPS and the BPP
have the same 24 groups of words to which the test
taker responds. In contrast to the test's brevity (one
page), the number of pages devoted to the number
of patterns that can result from the test is
amazing.[18] In the BPP there are over 30 individuals
listed from the Bible (from Abraham to the apostle
Paul) with their accompanying patterns.[19] To think
that responding to merely 24 groups of words in
three minutes (the time it took us to complete the
test) could yield that many patterns and be applied
to that many individuals in Scripture does stretch
the limits of credulity!

The PPS and the BPP are featured in Ken Voges and Ron Braund's book, *Understanding How Others Misunderstand You: A Unique and Proven Plan for Strengthening Personal Relationships*, which we discussed earlier. In view of the foregoing information, it is obvious that the title's implied promises are not scientifically defensible and that the admitted relationship to the four temperaments should, for biblical reasons, prohibit Christians from participating.

The director of Christian Financial Concepts is Larry Burkett. In his materials catalog there is a listing of the PPS which says:

> This is the self-scoring version of the DISC instrument that Larry Burkett began using years ago to determine a person's basic personality profile. With it you can identify your primary and secondary motivations and begin to understand the strengths and weaknesses of your personality. You can also learn to appreciate how others have different motivations and see how each profile has a most desired and most efficient work environment.[20]

The implied promises in this and other such listings are wholly incompatible with the facts.

Our recommendation for the PPS and the BPP is the same as for the MBTI. For both biblical and scientific reasons those two instruments should not be used to evaluate individuals for Christian service or for personal understanding.

Taylor-Johnson Temperament Analysis.

The Taylor-Johnson Temperament Analysis
(TJTA) is a personality inventory that does not
claim to be based upon any personality theory.
However, contained within it we see obvious similarities to Jungian theory found in both the MBTI
and the PPS. The TJTA provides the following nine
bipolar scales:

Nervous	—	Composed
Depressive	—	Light-hearted
Active-Social	—	Quiet
Expressive-Responsive	—	Inhibited
Sympathetic	—	Indifferent
Subjective	—	Objective
Dominant	—	Submissive
Hostile	—	Tolerant
Self-disciplined	—	Impulsive[21]

Psychological Publications, Inc., which prints
and distributes the TJTA says that TJTA test
scores were compared with psychologists' ratings
on the same individuals. They say, "Empirical
validity of the TJTA was first determined by using
professional clinical ratings." They also say, "In
most cases the predictions were closely duplicated
by the test results."[22]

In response to a letter of inquiry about the
empirical validity statement above, Psychological
Publications said in essence that the research
records were unavailable. The letter refers to the
procedure used as "a more or less informal survey."
The letter goes on to state that "the results were

compared with the staff's clinical impressions and findings."[23] There seems to be a discrepancy between the empirical validity reported in the TJTA manual and what was stated in the letter from Psychological Publications, Inc. We conclude that the empirical validity evidence has been over-reported and is presently not even verifiable.

As mentioned earlier, one of the most important information sources about tests is the *Mental Measurements Yearbook* (MMY). The *Tenth Mental Measurements Yearbook* says: "This reviewer's major reservation concerning the TJTA is the question of its validity." The reviewer says that "the main objective evidence for validity presented in the [TJTA] manual" is "certainly not sufficient to demonstrate test validity."[24]

H. Norman Wright, a pastor turned psychologist, heads Christian Marriage Enrichment (CME). For years Wright has been promoting the TJTA. The CME announcement refers to the TJTA as producing a profile that is "extremely useful in premarital, marital and individual counseling." The come-on litany is as follows:

> Have you ever been "stuck" in counseling?
> Have you wondered whether to work with a
>   person yourself or refer?
> Have you wanted a way to discover a
>   person's problems immediately without
>   taking ten hours of counseling time?
> Would you like to be able to use a
>   personality indicator both for counseling
>   & group Bible studies?

Would you like to know "What to do" in
counseling sessions?
Have you ever wanted to know how to help
someone struggling with worry, anger,
depression or negative self-talk?
If you have any "yes" answers, the TJTA
seminar is for you.[25]

To say the least, there is a discontinuity between
what academic literature reveals and the implied
promises in Wright's advertising.

While the TJTA is not as transparently related
to the four temperaments—and therefore to the
horoscope—there are some similarities. We are
concerned about these similarities. The TJTA is not
as easily condemned for its horoscopic connections,
but why use it if there is a possible connection?
While we cannot be as certain as we are for the
MBTI and the PPS that there may be a biblical
violation related to the four temperaments, we still
recommend—at least for scientific reasons—the
TJTA should not be used to evaluate individuals for
Christian service or for personal understanding.

LaHaye Temperament Analysis (LTA).

Dr. Tim LaHaye has shown a great desire to
help people determine their temperament type. In
addition to writing books on the subject, LaHaye
has created his own instruments. His book *Why
You Act the Way You Do* includes a do-it-yourself
Personal Profile Blob Chart with questions people
can ask themselves. Moreover, he has devised the
LaHaye Temperament Analysis.

In spite of LaHaye's assurance that his LTA is "over 92 percent accurate," there is no evidence for its accuracy. We looked extensively in the academic literature and found no listing for the LTA. This includes the *Mental Measurements Yearbook*, *Tests in Print*, the *Test Collection Bibliographies*, and various academic data bases. We shared this information with a University of California professor who specializes in testing and measurement. The man is not a Christian, but his response is interesting. He said, "I would estimate the validity of such tests to be somewhere between reading tea leaves and the I Ching." When we asked him what he meant by that, he said one should never trust any psychological test that had not been subjected to the usual critical reviews—including a look at its validity.

We found no reference to any validation studies done on the LTA by the usual academic procedures or in any of LaHaye's writings. Nevertheless, he says in *Why You Act the Way You Do*:

> I went on to develop my own tests which I administered to volunteers in my congregation, among my acquaintances, and to over one thousand missionaries encountered on a world missions tour. Finally, I came up with the LaHaye Temperament Analysis, which I believe is over 92 percent accurate. We have given it to almost 20,000 people and have received very few complaints. In fact, those who have taken the test are quite amazed at its thoroughness and professionalism.[26]

In academic circles validation by "very few complaints" would either evoke laughter or lamentation. Laughter because it would be academically laughable; lamentation because it would be academically ludicrous to use such a standard for test validation. There are standards by which tests are constructed, administered, and evaluated. A good text on this is *Standards for Educational and Psychological Testing*.[27] We would think that Christians would want to use the highest possible standards of proof before promoting ideas and tests in the manner done by LaHaye and others. If he has met the rigorous requirements and standards, we have seen no evidence of it.

Even if the LTA were to meet the academic standards, the ideology behind the test is not such that a Christian should have anything to do with it. Tests to determine the four temperaments are on the same spiritual level as charting the horoscope. We are simply bringing up the academic weaknesses of the LTA to demonstrate that it does not meet scientific requirements any more than it meets biblical requirements.

At the end of *Why You Act the Way You Do*, there are instructions on "How to get your personalized LaHaye Temperament Analysis." He makes the following promises:

> The LaHaye Temperament Analysis is the result of over fifteen years' research and is the most unique test of its kind available today. Each analysis is personally prepared and presented in a thirteen- to seventeen-

page letter from the author (depending on your temperament combination and other pastoral information). It will provide you with the following information in a keepsake leatherette binder which will be of interest to you for years to come.

1. Your primary and secondary temperament: The 92 percent accuracy level is extremely high. The standard IQ test is only considered 80 percent accurate.
2. Your vocational aptitudes, including at least fifty different vocations you could do comfortably.
3. An analysis of your three major vocational weaknesses with appropriate suggestions.
4. Your thirteen spiritual gifts in order of their priority, with an explanation for each.
5. Thirty vocations in your local church to which you are best suited.
6. Your ten major weaknesses, with appropriate suggestions on bringing them into control.
7. Positive personal suggestions on how to overcome your weaknesses.
8. If you're married, some suggestions on how to treat you mate.
9. If single, how to best face life as a single with your temperament combination.
10. If you are a parent, some suggestions on parenting for your type of temperament.[28]

We called and spoke with a woman in Dr. LaHaye's office and asked whether there is anything written concerning the research done on the LaHaye Temperament Analysis. She did not know and said she would return our call, which she did. She said Dr. LaHaye told her the research was done in San Diego 15 or more years ago and the details were not published. When asked if more information could be gained by writing to LaHaye, she said no. She said that all of the information is in the book.

Based upon our research and understanding of the standards for tests, we find that LaHaye has overpromised and overpromoted without the usual academic means of support for what he says and what he sells. For both biblical and academic reasons the LTA should not be used to evaluate individuals for Christian service or for personal understanding.

Personality Profile Test (PPT).

The Personality Profile Test (PPT) was devised by Florence Littauer. Her test falls into the same problems of unsubstantiation and lack of validity. Therefore we have almost the same comments for the PPT as for the LTA. We do not find it listed in the academic literature. Thus, it has probably not been validated. If such tests were biblical and depended on no other ideology, we would still require them to meet academic standards of integrity.

Littauer's book cover says: "Discover the real you by uncovering the roots of . . . *Your Personality Tree*." On the front of her book *Personality Plus* are the words, "How to understand others by understanding yourself," and "Special Feature: Personality Profile Test!" The implied promises for self knowledge are unsubstantiated by valid research. The PPT, like the LTA, is based upon the four temperaments. Therefore, for both biblical and academic reasons, the PPT should not be used by Christians.

The Lord has not instructed us to evaluate ourselves according to our personalities, but rather according to His Word. Taking personality tests turns one's focus towards self rather than towards God. We are to look into the perfect law of liberty in Christ. He is both our example and our enabling. Rather than wasting time on taking personality tests that have not even measured up to academic standards of validity, Christians should be spending time learning the Word of God and practicing obedience. If one were to make a point of daily following the outline given in 2 Timothy 3:16-17, one would be far better off. Moreover, he would be glorifying the Lord rather than himself.

> All scripture is given by inspiration of God, and is profitable for doctrine, for reproof, for correction, for instruction in righteousness: that the man of God may be perfect, thoroughly furnished unto all good works.

Spiritual Gifts Inventories.

Perhaps worse than the two areas of testing that we have discussed (personality and temperament) is the idea that a test or inventory would reveal a Christian's spiritual gifts. The "Spiritual Gifts Inventory" and its accompanying guide "Understanding Spiritual Gifts" comprise just one of numerous inventories and tests used to discover one's spiritual gifts.[29]

The idea behind the inventories is the same as behind career tests—personality traits and types match certain activities and preferences. Line up the traits, preferences, and activities and you end up with a possible career choice. Such tests reduce spiritual gifts and service in the Body of Christ to career interest inventories and a job in the marketplace.

Since those who create and promote such tests are copying the business world, they at least ought to follow the academic guidelines for validation. In none of these inventories have we seen anything resembling the minimum requirements needed for a statistically valid instrument. People are looking to an unproven, extrabiblical instrument to determine God's will and God's call to service. However, the lack of statistical validity is not the most serious problem with using spiritual gifts inventories.

In essence such inventories deny Paul's declaration that he was "made a minister, according to the gift of the grace of God given unto me by the effectual working of his power" (Ephesians 3:7). Was he made a minister "according to the gift of the grace of God given unto me by the effectual working of his power" or by his natural personality traits?

If people are following career-choice types of inventories to learn how to fit into the Body of Christ, they may be serving from the wrong power base (personality "strengths") and their own self-interests, rather than from the "effectual working" of God's power and from obedience to His will and plan.

While God may indeed use a person's natural talents for His service, He is not limited to that. Nor is He limited to using His children according to any pagan temperament type. He is sovereign and may sanctify natural talents into spiritual gifts. He may also curb the use of natural talents to prevent pride from swallowing the soul. He may also endue people with power that goes far beyond their natural abilities and inclinations. While people like to think that God used Paul because of his natural talents, Paul counted all that he was and had according to the flesh "dung." He knew the power of the resurrection of Christ indwelling him for service.

How did the Church throughout the ages, from its inception, ever function without these inventories? Very well! Spiritual gifts were recognized and exercised totally without the help of the modern-day testing movement and the penchant to worship numbers. The gifts are spiritual, not mathematical! They cannot be identified by psychological instruments except in the most superficial and erroneous way.

Although we mention one of the spiritual gifts inventories by name, we are not singling that one out as any worse than the rest. We are opposed to the use of all such tests and inventories that purport to identify spiritual gifts. While the Bible does not speak to the issue of such tests, it does warn us about following "philosophy and vain deceit, after the tradition of men, after the rudiments of the world, and not after Christ" (Colossians 2:8). Rather than using the ways of the world to identify spiritual gifts and callings, the New Testament believers resorted to prayer and guidance by the Holy Spirit.

Pastors have told us that spiritual gift inventories are useful to get their people to serve. They use the devices to motivate people to serve. However, to use an instrument that purports to identify spiritual gifts when there is a high probability for error, since there has been no validation of results, is dishonest.

Truth is too important an issue in the Body of Christ. Furthermore, what happens when an inventory gives someone the idea that he can (yea, should!) serve in a particular way that would be detrimental to the Body of Christ? What if the person is aggressive and demands to hold a particular position based upon his test performance? Getting a high score on any gift is no reason for a person to be placed in a particular ministry, since there is no proven validity to the results.

Spiritual gifts inventories may lead people not only to serve in the flesh, but also to depend upon their natural "strengths" rather than on the Lord in the process of serving Him. There is also the danger of focusing on self and self's gifts rather than on the Lord who is the Giver of gifts. For both biblical and academic reasons, we strongly recommend against the use of all such spiritual gifts inventories.

Personality Tests in the Church.

The use of various personality tests is becoming prolific among Christians. Those preparing for the pastorate and missionary work are often required to take such tests. As a result of such tests, many have been rejected from such service. However, we find nothing in the research literature that would warrant such a conclusion.

In his article "The Trouble with Testing," Martin Lasden quotes George Dudley, a test researcher and president of Behavioral Science Research Press of Dallas:

> Testing is a way to get at the truth sideways, and if you believe that the only way to get at the truth about another person is to administer a test, then you're not only fooling yourself, but you're also demonstrating a very negative view of mankind. You're saying that truth cannot be determined by asking the subject, or those who know the subject, but only by asking a testing expert.[30]

Dudley believes there should be more humility about testing.

Consider a man preparing for the mission field with a well-known and highly respected missionary organization. He was given one of the well-known personality tests. On the basis of the results, he was rejected from service. This is one of thousands of examples of personality testing at its worst. While one can only speculate, it does raise a question as to what would have happened to the great missionaries of the past if they had been subjected to taking personality tests before going to the mission field. God only knows! No one should ever be rejected from the pastorate or from missionary work on the basis of a personality test score or even on a battery of personality tests.

11

Why All the Deception?

Why are people—even Christians—running after personality inventories, temperament tests, and spiritual gifts inventories? Here are a few possible reasons.

1. The Barnum Effect.

Research reveals that individuals are very prone to accept the most general character descriptions as being specifically applicable to themselves. The term given to this phenomenon is the *Barnum Effect*, named after P. T. Barnum, who believed that a good circus had "a little something for everybody." Even though the descriptions or descriptive terms in the inventories, typologies, and tests apply equally well to other people, individuals are gullible enough to believe they are unique to themselves. Of course, this is exactly what happens with the horoscope, palm reading, and crystal ball gazing. This is known in research literature as the illusion of uniqueness and occurs at least for positive traits.[1]

In his article "Acceptance of Personality Test Results," Philippe Thiriart asks, "Is the accuracy of the results of a personality test an important factor in its acceptance by a psychologist's client?" After conducting an experiment and evaluating the results, Thiriart says:

> These findings indicate that people are more willing to accept socially desirable statements about themselves than those that are scientifically accurate. The findings also suggest why many people easily accept statements about their personality that come from astrologers and palm readers.[2]

2. Promotion by Popular Christians.

The personality inventories, temperament typologies, and tests of spiritual gifts are often promoted by well-known Christians. H. Norman Wright promotes the TJTA; Larry Burkett, Ken Voges, and Ron Braund promote the PPS; Tim LaHaye and Florence Littauer promote the four temperaments along with their own temperament tests; and many in the church endorse the MBTI. The promoters' popularity tends to cancel discernment by the user. After all, if H. Norman Wright promotes the TJTA it must be great. Also, these

promoters so often do it with such infectious enthusiasm. Unfortunately infectious enthusiasm by a
popular Christian for such products is enough to
overcome any reluctance.

3. Customer Enthusiasm.

The National Research Council warns against
personal experience and testimonials and says
these "are not regarded as an acceptable alternative to rigorous scientific evidence." The Council
goes on to say:

> Even when they have high face validity,
> such personal beliefs are not trustworthy
> as evidence. They often fail to consider the
> full range of factors that may be responsi-
> ble for an observed effect. Personal versions
> of reality, which are essentially private, are
> especially antithetical to science, which is a
> fundamentally public enterprise.[3]

Personal experiences and testimonials, as important as they are to individuals expressing them,
do not constitute scientific proof. LaHaye, Littauer,
Voges and Braund all have personal experiences
and testimonials to support their promotion of what
they do; however, they lack scientific proof.

In his book *The Inflated Self*, Dr. David Myers
says this about personality tests:

> People's believing horoscope data about
> themselves in the same way as personality
> test data, and their being most receptive to

> personality test feedback on tests that have
> the lowest actual validity, raises some dis-
> concerting implications for psychiatry and
> clinical psychology. Regardless of whether
> a particular diagnosis has any validity, the
> recipient is likely to stand in awe of it,
> especially after expending effort and money
> to receive it.[4]

There is a tendency to support a system in
which one has invested time and money, even if the
money is only the cost of a book. Unfortunately, the
test user who becomes committed is the main
source of others being enticed. The enthusiastic
user becomes the enthusiastic promoter, often
merely parroting the enthusiasm of the original
promoter. It may be that the real Barnum Effect is
Barnum's comment, "There's a sucker born every
minute."

4. The Illusion of Efficacy.

How do these popular Christians get to be such
believers in the first place? Myers tells how the
illusion of efficacy happens in psychotherapy:

> In experimental studies, therapists have
> tended to take credit for good outcomes, but
> not for poor outcomes. Hence, the clinician
> may surmise, "I helped Mr. X get better.
> But, despite my help, Mrs. Y got worse."[5]

Because it is natural to take credit for success and
to avoid blame for failure, an "illusion of efficacy"

occurs. Another facet of the illusion of efficacy is described by Myers. He says:

> Since people tend to seek help when things have hit bottom, any activity that is then undertaken may seem to be effective—both to the client and the therapist.[6]

The illusion of efficacy is so strong in the area of personality inventories that even when tests are known to lack proper validity, people will still use them because they still think they work. Once a person takes a test for a counselor, for instance, the counselor will look at the person through test results and will also look for and remember any confirming evidence.

After we spoke on testing at a conference and had mentioned our concerns with the Personal Profile System, an individual who had used the test for years told us that it was immaterial to him whether the test was valid or not. However, he said that he would be concerned if there were any connection between the PPS and the horoscope.

While we agree that his major concern should be its relationship to the horoscope, his additional concern should have been its validity. It sounded as if it didn't matter to him how invalid the test was as long as it wasn't related to the horoscope. Nevertheless, truth is too important to Christianity to ignore the validity of a testing instrument being used by Christians on Christians.

Summing up, "taking credit for good outcomes" and people improving supposedly after taking a test that gives them a new revelation, we see the power of the illusion of efficacy, which results in support for tests that should be rejected.

5. Illusory Correlation.
Myers says:

> Our confusion concerning correlation-causation is often compounded by our susceptibility to perceiving correlation where none exists. When we expect to see significant relationships, we easily misperceive random events as significantly related.[7]

He also says that "experiments indicate that people easily misperceive random events as confirming their beliefs."[8] If we have a certain label on ourselves and expect to behave in a certain way, our expectations will interpret our actions to conform to the label and therefore confirm it.

6. Self-Deception.
The Bible says, "The heart is deceitful above all things, and desperately wicked: who can know it?" (Jeremiah 17:9). Research does support the self-deception of individuals. We know that it is very common for people to distort reality and to have very inaccurate perceptions of themselves, their world (environment), and the future. Dr. Shelley Taylor's *Positive Illusions: Creative Self-Deception and the Healthy Mind* documents research that demonstrates how individuals are deceived about themselves, their environments, and their futures.

Much of this self-deception can so easily be carried over into personality inventories, temperament tests, and spiritual gifts inventories.

This is not a matter of faking; it is a matter of communicating our own self-deceptions while filling out the inventory or taking the test. For example, a person may think of himself as a great leader and aspire for leadership in a church. He takes a test for spiritual gifts and would naturally communicate this on the test. However, in reality he might be the worst possible choice as a leader. But once having communicated his self-deception on the test and finding a confirmation there, he becomes an ardent test promoter.

7. Self-Fulfilling Prophecy.

Dr. Robert Merton, in his book *Social Theory and Social Structure*, conceptualized the self-fulfilling prophecy.[9] Merton says the self-fulfilling prophecy occurs when "a false definition of [a] situation evokes a new behavior which makes the original conception come true." In other words, we tend to act in ways consistent with our expectations, even if they are not accurate.

Len Sandler, in an article on the self-fulfilling prophecy, says:

> It boils down to this: Consciously or not, we tip people off as to what our expectations are. We exhibit thousands of cues, some as subtle as the tilting of heads, the raising of eyebrows or the dilation of nostrils, but most are much more obvious. And people

pick up on those cues. The concept of the self-fulfilling prophecy can be summarized in five key principles:

1. We form certain expectations of people or events.
2. We communicate those expectations with various cues.
3. People tend to respond to these cues by adjusting their behavior to match them.
4. The result is that the original expectation becomes true.
5. This creates a circle of self-fulfilling prophecies.[10]

Parents can easily fall into the trap of eliciting certain behavior from their children by expecting them to act in a certain way. For instance, a mother may have been told that her little boy is a perfect Choleric according to a test. She may consequently expect aggressive behavior. Every child displays some aggressive behavior, but since his mother has tagged him as Choleric, she is overly sensitized to any aggressive behavior. She may think she is handling the situation well by accepting aggressiveness, because she expects his angry outbursts. But, she may well be encouraging them through both her expectation and her subtle acceptance of that behavior now that she "understands" his temperament. If she doesn't already have a little Choleric, she will create one.

8. Illusory Thinking.

Fallacious thinking is something we are all involved in, and it's generally easier to catch someone else at it than ourselves. Knowing our attitude about personality testing, a man spoke with us about some consulting he had done for the local police department in that city. He said he had tested 100 successful policemen to see what commonality existed. He then set up a personality profile based upon the results. New police force applicants whose profiles were similar to those of the successful policemen were admitted to police training; those with dissimilar profiles were rejected. He asked what we thought of what he did and we explained to him the following problems:

1. The test provides a snapshot of what the policemen were like **at the point of success** rather than what these same men's profiles may have looked like when they originally applied for police training.
2. **No double blind study** had been set up to let in a group of men who did not fit the profile. They should admit such a group and then check their future success and compare it with those who did fit the profile and were accepted.
3. The commonality or profile of successful policemen may be a **commonality of weaknesses** rather than strengths. Their strengths may be so individual and different from one another that no profile could capture them.
4. Self-fulfilling prophecy could be involved here.

9. Numerolatry.

Many people are involved in a sort of numerolatry (number worship). If a test utilizes numbers and numerical profiles, it is assumed that it must therefore be scientific and valid. The use of numbers, mathematics, statistics, correlations, and measures of significance do not mean that the end result (a test score) is valid. Few people realize that even when a test has been shown to be statistically significant, that the statistical significance is often so small that it is really insignificant.

While the lack of validity should silence the zealous Christian promoters of personality inventories and temperament tests, it hasn't even dampened their enthusiasm. Promotion and use of such inventories and tests is a testimony to the naivete and negligence of many Christians.

12

Christ in You:
the Hope of Glory

Biblical Categories of Individual Differences.
Individual differences of temperament and personality can make life interesting and challenging. But, the Bible does not categorize people according to temperament or personality. Instead, the richness of variety permeates the pages of God's Word. There were nations and genealogies, but there were no temperament types. God used fascinating people to show forth His glory and accomplish His purposes, but they were not temperament types.

Biblical classifications of people are always in terms of their relationship to God. These are the kinds of classifications that Christians should be interested in. Psalm 1 sets forth two types of people:

Blessed is the man that walketh not in the counsel of the ungodly, nor standeth in the way of sinners, nor sitteth in the seat of the scornful.

But his delight is in the law of the LORD; and in His law doth he meditate day and night.

And he shall be like a tree planted by the rivers of water, that bringeth forth his fruit in his season; his leaf also shall not wither; and whatsoever he doeth shall prosper.

The ungodly are not so: but are like the chaff which the wind driveth away.

Therefore the ungodly shall not stand in the judgment, nor sinners in the congregation of the righteous.

For the LORD knoweth the way of the righteous: but the way of the ungodly shall perish.

The distinction is not made according to introversion or extroversion, or according to whether a person is analytical or emotional. The distinction is made on the basis of whether a person walks in obedience or sin, whether he is godly or ungodly. And, that distinction is a matter of eternal life or death.

Classifications in the Bible between the godly
and the ungodly, the saved and the lost, and
between babes in Christ and mature believers have
been created by God. God uses those distinctions to
call a people to Himself so that once again His
image might be reflected as He purposed from the
beginning.

Even with all kinds of wonderful temperament
or personality traits, if a person is among the lost,
he is described this way:

> . . . dead in trespasses and sins . . .
> fulfilling the desires of the flesh and of the
> mind . . . by nature the children of wrath
> (Ephesians 2:1-3).

> Gentiles in the flesh . . . without Christ,
> being aliens from the commonwealth of
> Israel, and strangers from the covenants of
> promise, having no hope, and without God
> in the world (Ephesians 2:11-12).

> Having the understanding darkened, being
> alienated from the life of God through the
> ignorance that is in them, because of the
> blindness of their heart: Who being past
> feeling have given themselves over unto
> lasciviousness, to work all uncleanness
> with greediness (Ephesians 4:18-19).

From the moment of new birth, God begins His
work of transforming an individual according to His
perfect plan. He has given His Word, His Holy

Spirit, and all that is necessary for life and godliness.

> Grace and peace be multiplied unto you through the knowledge of God, and of Jesus our Lord, according as his divine power hath given unto us all things that pertain unto life and godliness, through the knowledge of him that hath called us to glory and virtue: whereby are given unto us exceeding great and precious promises: that by these ye might be partakers of the divine nature, having escaped the corruption that is in the world through lust (2 Peter 1:2-4).

Notice that the Lord does not have Peter say, "Add virtues to your temperament strengths." Instead, he says:

> And beside this, giving all diligence, add to your faith virtue; and to virtue knowledge; and to knowledge temperance; and to temperance patience; and to patience godliness; and to godliness brotherly kindness; and to brotherly kindness charity (2 Peter 1:5-7).

The only classification given in this next passage has to do with those who respond to the life of Christ in them and those who have forgotten what God has done:

> For if these things be in you, and abound, they make you that ye shall neither be

barren nor unfruitful in the knowledge of
our Lord Jesus Christ. But he that lacketh
these things is blind, and cannot see afar
off, and hath forgotten that he was purged
from his old sins (2 Peter 1:8-9).

Peter does not say, "Identify your temperament
strengths and weaknesses and add the temperament traits of the Spirit." Instead he says:

Wherefore the rather, brethren, give
diligence to make your calling and election
sure: for if ye do these things, ye shall
never fall: for so an entrance shall be
ministered unto you abundantly into the
everlasting kingdom of our Lord and
Saviour Jesus Christ (2 Peter 1:10-11).

Christianity is a very personal relationship
with Jesus Christ. It is not a religious system of
formulas or fabrications of man-made means for
self-improvement. When a person is born again by
the sovereign will of God (John 1:12-13), he
becomes a new creation in Christ. The Holy Spirit
comes to indwell him and to conform him into the
image of Jesus Christ. God works from the inside
through His Word and His Spirit. He also uses
circumstances in believers' lives to conform them to
His image (Romans 8:28-29). The Christian's part
is to respond to what God is doing through Spirit-
enabled obedience. He becomes more like Christ as
he focuses on God rather than on self.

> But we all, with open face beholding as in a
> glass the glory of the Lord, are changed
> into the same image from glory to glory,
> even as by the Spirit of the Lord (2
> Corinthians 3:18).

Freedom from Bondage.

Personality typologies and tests put people under bondage to worldly systems and standards. Each psychological system presents a theory to explain the human condition, describes how they should be, and presents a method of change. Thus each system condemns people through a man-made standard of judgment concerning how they should be, and each system presents a plan and promises for change.

Once a person buys into such a system, he vainly attempts to become what that system promises he can be. It is a never-ending cycle of works with users always trying to reach the standard, but never quite making it. That is why people tend to go from one psychological system of change to another, from one therapy to another.

Not one of them gives all it promises. The same is true of typologies like the four temperaments, DiSC, and the enneagram. Each is a system that offers freedom to become one's very best. In reality, each is a form of bondage.

The apostle Paul was concerned with any philosophy or religious activity that contaminated the pure Gospel of grace. His letter to the Galatians expresses his concern about the seriousness of adding works that pervert the Gospel of Christ:

> I marvel that ye are so soon removed from
> him that called you into the grace of Christ
> unto another gospel: which is not another;
> but there be some that trouble you, and
> would pervert the gospel of Christ. But
> though we, or an angel from heaven,
> preach any other gospel unto you than that
> which we have preached unto you, let him
> be accursed. As we said before, so say I now
> again, If any man preach any other gospel
> unto you than that ye have received, let
> him be accursed (Galatians 1:6-9).

Paul called any addition to the Gospel of Christ
"another gospel" that would "pervert the gospel of
Christ." Whatever has to do with matters of the
soul that adds to the Gospel of grace will compete
with and contaminate the pure Word of God. For
the Christians, the most dangerous additions are
those that are mixed with Bible references.

During Paul's day, the Judaizers said faith in
Christ by the Gospel was not enough. They taught
that followers of Christ had to be circumcised to
assure their salvation. Paul was not opposed to circumcision itself, but rather to those who were
enticing people to become circumcised just in case
faith in Jesus was not enough. Judaizers under-
mined the finished work of Christ and urged people
to do something to establish their standing before
God. They were, in fact, denying the efficacy of the
Cross for initial salvation.

Today, the works added to the Cross of Christ
are not circumcision. Instead of adding circumci-

sion to faith in Christ, countless Christians are adding the works of self-improvement through psychological systems, such as the four temperaments and other typologies. Thus, they are denying the efficacy of the Cross in terms of sanctification. Countless Christians are trusting in self-improvement formulas along with or instead of trusting fully in the sufficiency of God's provisions for living the Christian life. In so doing, they are saying that Jesus' death and resurrection are inadequate, that God's grace is insufficient, that God's Word is incomplete, that the Holy Spirit needs "another helper," and that the Gospel is limited to saving us from the final judgment.

Today, mere psychological opinions of men are being added to the Cross of Christ and the Gospel of grace. The situation is much like in the Old Testament when the Israelites were incorporating the surrounding nations' idolatry. The Lord grieved over the people who turned away from His absolute sufficiency:

> Hath a nation changed their gods, which are yet no gods? but my people have changed their glory for that which doth not profit. Be astonished, O ye heavens, at this, and be horribly afraid, be ye very desolate, saith the LORD. For my people have committed two evils; they have forsaken me the fountain of living waters, and hewed them out cisterns, broken cisterns, that can hold no water (Jeremiah 2:11-13).

Today, rather than trusting God to complete
the work He has begun in every true Christian,
many are attempting to become better Christians
through secular and pagan psychological methods.

The Way of Death and the Way of Life.

After arguing that "man is not justified by the
works of the law, but by the faith of Jesus Christ"
(Galatians 2:16), Paul emphasizes the drastic sepa-
ration between attempting to secure one's own righteousness and trusting the grace of God. *Death* and
resurrection are the only words that can describe
the radical difference. And, indeed, the new life in
Christ comes only by His death and by our identification with that death. He died in the place of who
we were and gave us new life to replace that old
life.

Henceforth we are not to live by that old life. It
is to be counted dead (Romans 6). We are not to try
to analyze it or improve it. Instead, we are to live
by the new life in Christ Jesus. Thus Paul's description of himself is not exclusively for him or specially
for mature believers. These words are for every
Christian:

> I am crucified with Christ: nevertheless I
> live; yet not I, but Christ liveth in me: and
> the life which I now live in the flesh I live
> by the faith of the Son of God, who loved
> me, and gave himself for me (Galatians
> 2:20).

Paul did **not** say, "the life which I now live in the flesh I live by the faith of the Son of God" **plus** the four temperaments or **plus** any other psychological system for understanding and changing people. In fact, he called the Galatians foolish for adding anything to faith in the finished work of Christ:

> O foolish Galatians, who hath bewitched you, that ye should not obey the truth, before whose eyes Jesus Christ hath been evidently set forth, crucified among you? This only would I learn of you, received ye the Spirit by the works of the law, or by the hearing of faith? Are ye so foolish? having begun in the Spirit, are ye now made perfect by the flesh? (Galatians 3:1-3).

And this is exactly what so many Christians are tempted to do. "Having begun in the Spirit" they are trying to be "made perfect by the flesh" through psychological means.

Identification with Jesus.

Rather than teaching us to focus on personality and temperament, God is transforming us into the image of Christ through the Holy Spirit. He describes what we are to become through His Word, He demonstrates the way we are to live through Christ and saintly examples, but He does more than that. He works through the inside, because he has infused His life and character into us through

His Holy Spirit. He gives us His external, written, living Word and His internal, living Word through the Spirit.

The believer's identification in Christ sets him free to love and obey the Lord according to the very life of Christ and the very truth of Christ. Jesus promises:

> If ye continue in my word, then are ye my disciples indeed; and ye shall know the truth, and the truth shall make you free (John 8:31-32).

Paul explains our freedom in Christ in his letter to the Romans:

> There is therefore now no condemnation to them which are in Christ Jesus, who walk not after the flesh, but after the Spirit. For the law of the Spirit of life in Christ Jesus hath made me free from the law of sin and death. For what the law could not do, in that it was weak through the flesh, God sending his own Son in the likeness of sinful flesh, and for sin, condemned sin in the flesh: That the righteousness of the law might be fulfilled in us, who walk not after the flesh, but after the Spirit (Romans 8:1-4).

If the law of God, which is holy, cannot make us "free from sin," how can any other religious, philosophical, or psychological system do so? If the perfect law of God was "weak through the flesh," why do Christians look for another system of "laws"? That is what personality typologies are. They are man-made laws of who is what and why and how. God has provided the only way to overcome the flesh and that was by sending His Son to die in our place—to "condemn sin in the flesh." Psychological systems leave us in our sins, but the Son sets us free!

Because of our freedom in Christ, Paul urges:

> Stand fast therefore in the liberty wherewith Christ hath made us free, and be not entangled again with the yoke of bondage (Galatians 5:1).

However, we are not set free to be me and to do my own thing. Instead we are free to live our new life in Jesus—not to reach our highest potential, but to become like Jesus to love and to serve.

> For, brethren, ye have been called unto liberty; only use not liberty for an occasion to the flesh, but by love serve one another (Galatians 5:13).

God's plan for us to "not fulfill the lust of the flesh" is for us to walk in the Spirit—that is, by His indwelling and enabling presence (Galatians 5:16). Walking in the Spirit is allowing Christ to live His life in and through us. All other methods of overcoming "weaknesses" only rearrange, strengthen and feed the flesh.

Spiritual Warfare.

Why, then, is there so much seeming failure in the Christian life? Why are so many Christians looking for answers outside the Word of God and outside the provisions promised in His Word? Perhaps there's a misunderstanding about what it means to be a Christian in terms of His life at work in us. Perhaps some have forgotten that there is a warfare going on, or they haven't learned to do battle against the world, the flesh, and the devil. Rather than learning to wage battle in spiritual warfare with the sword of the Spirit—the Word of God—and with the shield of faith, many Christians have entered enemy territory looking for other ways to improve their condition.

Paul continues his letter to the Galatians with a description of the battle between the flesh and the Spirit:

> For the flesh lusteth against the Spirit, and the Spirit against the flesh: and these are contrary the one to the other: so that ye cannot do the things that ye would (Galatians 5:18).

The only way to victory is to be led by the Spirit. As Paul says, "But if ye be led of the Spirit, ye are not under the law" (Galatians 5:18). The key is to be led by the Spirit, but that requires one to die to self and that is where the resistance lies.

How many of us still want to hang onto our old ways? How many of us clutch some cherished part of what we once were? God's ways require His

sovereignty in our lives. Do we resist Him to be
Sovereign Lord, King of Kings, Master, and Owner
because we've been our own little gods for so long?
Is it because we've been strengthening our flesh
through extrabiblical self-improvement programs?

Rather than teaching us to find out what temperament or personality type we are and to use our
strengths and overcome our weaknesses, the Bible
reveals that we are in a spiritual battle between
the flesh (our old life) and the Spirit (His life in us).
When the flesh wins a skirmish the works of the
flesh will be manifest:

> Now the works of the flesh are manifest,
> which are these; adultery, fornication, un-
> cleanness, lasciviousness, idolatry, witch-
> craft, hatred, variance, emulations, wrath,
> strife, seditions, heresies, envyings, mur-
> ders, drunkenness, revellings, and such
> like: of the which I tell you before, as I have
> also told you in time past, that they which
> do such things shall not inherit the king-
> dom of God (Galatians 5:19-21).

But when the Christian is walking in the Spirit
and being led by the Spirit, the fruit of the Spirit
will be manifest:

> But the fruit of the Spirit is love, joy, peace,
> longsuffering, gentleness, goodness, faith,
> meekness, temperance: against such there
> is no law (Galatians 5:22-23).

The fruit of the Spirit are not temperament traits of the new man; they are manifestations of the Holy Spirit. They are essentially different from those similar traits of natural man, because they are the result of the indwelling Holy Spirit. The fruit of the Spirit is evidence of Christ in you, the hope of glory!

The spiritual battle was initially won at the Cross. Therefore Paul declares:

> And they that are Christ's have crucified the flesh with the affections and lusts. If we live in the Spirit, let us also walk in the Spirit (Galatians 5:24-25).

Paul describes walking in the Spirit in Romans 8 as well. One key element that applies to the error of using personality theories is this:

> For they that are after the flesh do mind the things of the flesh; but they that are after the Spirit the things of the Spirit. For to be carnally minded is death; but to be spiritually minded is life and peace (Romans 8:5-6).

Temperament and personality typologies cause people to "mind the things of the flesh." Even though one of LaHaye's purposes for using the four temperaments was to encourage people to walk in the Spirit, such a plan contradicts the clear Word of God. We do not become more spiritual through minding the things of the flesh.

Christ has given Christians His righteousness. They need not establish their own. Nor can they attain their own righteousness though any kind of psychological system of self-knowledge or self-improvement. God is the One who works in believers through His Word and His Spirit to conform them into the image of Christ. There is no need to use the wisdom of men.

> For the word of God is quick, and powerful, and sharper than any twoedged sword, piercing even to the dividing asunder of soul and spirit, and of the joints and marrow, and is a discerner of the thoughts and intents of the heart. Neither is there any creature that is not manifest in his sight: but all things are naked and opened unto the eyes of him with whom we have to do (Hebrews 4:12-13).

The Lord, the discerner of hearts, sees what needs to be changed. And, believers do not have to hide from their own sin, because Christ Jesus is their High Priest.

> Seeing then that we have a great high priest, that is passed into the heavens, Jesus the Son of God, let us hold fast our profession. For we have not an high priest which cannot be touched with the feeling of our infirmities; but was in all points tempted like as we are, yet without sin (Hebrews 4:14-15).

And through all of this He is conforming us into His own image, "that he might be the firstborn among many brethren" (Romans 8:29).

The Lord knows each person's individual uniqueness. He knows how many hairs are on the head of each person at any given time. And He knows the exact genetic makeup of every person born on this planet. Nevertheless, in His Word He did not set forth a system for understanding temperament traits. Nor did He set forth a plan by which people could analyze the strengths and weaknesses of their temperaments or personalities in order to find success and happiness.

Instead, He gave us His Word and His Son. He gave us new life to enable us to live in love and obedience to Him. His work in a person and that person's response of love and obedience will bring out the beauty of individual differences to reflect His glory in a unique and living way. The Bible's focus is not the mystery of individual differences of temperament and personality. The biblical focus is Jesus Christ and the mystery of Christ in you, the hope of glory!

Notes

Chapter 1: Christians and the Four Temperaments

1. Tim LaHaye. *Why You Act the Way You Do*. Wheaton: Tyndale House Publishers, Inc., 1984, front cover of the Living Books Edition.
2. Hans Eysenck. *Fact and Fiction in Psychology*. Baltimore: Penguin Books, 1965, p. 56.
3. John Ankerberg and John Weldon. *Astrology: Do the Heavens Rule Our Destiny?* Eugene, OR: Harvest House Publishers, p. 189.
4. Peter Glick, "Stars In Our Eyes." *Psychology Today*, August 1987, p. 6.

Chapter 2: Occult Origins of the Four Temperaments

1. R. W. Lundin, "Humoral Theory." *Encyclopedia of Psychology*, Volume 2. Raymond Corsini, ed. New York: John Wiley & Sons, 1984, p.167.
2. Felix M. Cleve. *The Giants of Pre-Sophistic Greek Philosophy: An Attempt to Reconstruct Their Thoughts*, Vol. 2. The Hague, Netherlands: Martinus Nijhoff, 1965, pp. 342-343.
3. Louis MacNeice. *Astrology*. London: Bloomsbury Books, 1989, p. 120.
4. Lundin, *op. cit.*, p. 167.
5. Edwin Burton Levine. *Hippocrates*. New York: Twayne Publishers, Inc., 1971, p. 46.
6. K. J. Shapiro, "Mental Illness: Early History." *Encyclopedia of Psychology*, Volume 2. Raymond Corsini, ed. New York: John Wiley & Sons, 1984, p. 360.

7. *The Dialogues of Plato*, Vol. 2. B. Jowett, trans. New York: Random House, 1937, p. 63.
8. *Ibid.*
9. *Ibid.*
10. Rudolph E. Siegel. *Galen on Psychology, Psychopathology, and Function and Diseases of the Nervous System*. New York: S. Karger, 1973, p. 174.
11. Stanley W. Jackson. *Melancholia and Depression: From Hippocratic Times to Modern Times*. New Haven: Yale University Press, 1986, p. 5.
12. Shapiro, *op. cit.*, p. 361.
13. Lundin, *op. cit.*, p. 167.
14. Siegel, *op. cit.*, p. 178.
15. Henry Sigerist. *A History of Medicine*. New York: Oxford University Press, 1961, p. 322.
16. R. W. Coan, "Personality Types." *Encyclopedia of Psychology*, Volume 3. Raymond Corsini, ed. New York: John Wiley & Sons, 1984, p. 24.
17. Lynn Thorndike. *Magic and Experimental Science*, Vol. 1. New York: Columbia University Press, 1923, pp. 178-179.
18. C. G. Jung. *Psychological Types*. Princeton, NJ: Princeton University Press, 1971, p. 531.
19. K. J. Shapiro, "Temperaments." *Encyclopedia of Psychology*, Volume 3. Raymond Corsini, ed. New York: John Wiley & Sons, 1984, p. 410.
20. Frederick B. Artz. *The Mind of the Middle Ages*, 2nd Edition. New York: Knopf, 1954, pp. 236-237.
21. J. H. Robinson quoted in *An Intellectual and Cultural History of the Western World*, Vol. 1. Harry Elmer Barnes. New York: Dover Publications, 1937, p. 428.
22. Judith S. Neaman. *Suggestion of the Devil: The Origins of Madness*. Garden City: Anchor Press/Doubleday, 1975 , p. 8.

Chapter 3: Astrology and the Four Temperaments

1. John Ankerberg and John Weldon. *Astrology: Do the Heavens Rule Our Destiny?* Eugene, OR: Harvest House Publishers, 1989, p. 51.

2. Fred Gettings. *Dictionary of Astrology*. Boston: Routledge & Kegan Paul, 1985, p. 125.
3. *Ibid.*, p. 106.
4. *Ibid.*, p. 197.
5. *Ibid.*, p. 7.
6. *Ibid.*, pp. 136-137.
7. *Ibid.*, p. 348.
8. *Ibid.*, p. 237.
9. Ankerberg and Weldon, *op. cit.*, p. 51.
10. *Ibid.*, p. 68.
11. *Ibid.*, p. 69.
12. *Ibid.*, p. 81.
13. *Ibid.*, pp. 81-82.
14. *Ibid.*
15. *Ibid.*, p. 102.
16. *Ibid.*, pp. 102-103.
17. *Ibid.*, p. 189.
18. *Ibid.*, p. 113.
19. *Ibid.*, p. 294.
20. *Ibid.*, pp. 295-296.
21. Gettings, *op. cit.*, p. 131.
22. *Ibid.*, pp. 256-257.
23. W. E. Vine. *The Expanded Vine's Expository Dictionary of the New Testament*. Minneapolis: Bethany House Publishers, 1984, p. 352.
24. *Ibid.*, pp. 352-353.

Chapter 4: Temperament Teachers

1. Tim LaHaye. *Why You Act the Way You Do*. Tyndale House Publishers, Inc., 1984, p. 9.
2. *Ibid.*, p. 58.
3. *Ibid.*, p. 59.
4. Ole Hallesby. *Temperament and the Christian Faith*. Minneapolis: Augsburg Publishing House, 1962.
5. Tim LaHaye. *Spirit-Controlled Temperament*. Wheaton, IL: Tyndale House, 1666, 1967 edition, p. 4.
6. Hans J. Eysenck. *Fact and Fiction in Psychology*. Baltimore: Penguin Books, 1965.
7. *Ibid.*, p. 54.

8. Tim LaHaye. *Transformed Temperaments*. Wheaton, IL: Tyndale House Publishers, 1971.
9. *Ibid.*, p. 10.
10. Eysenck, *op. cit.*, pp. 55-57.
11. LaHaye, *Why You Act the Way You Do*, *op. cit.*, p. 14.
12. Adrian Furnham. "Write or Wrong: The Validity of Graphological Analysis," *The Skeptical Inquirer*, Vol. 13, No. 1, Fall 1988, pp. 64-69.
13. LaHaye, *Transformed Temperaments*, *op. cit.*, p. 16.
14. LaHaye, *Spirit-Controlled Temperament*, *op. cit.*, p. 4.
15. *Ibid.*, pp. 24-42.
16. *Ibid.*, p. 112.
17. *Ibid.*, p. 70.
18. *Ibid.*, p. 5.
19. *Ibid.*
20. *Ibid.*, p. 6.
21. *Ibid.*
22. LaHaye, *Why You Act the Way You Do*, *op. cit.*, p. 9.
23. *Ibid.*, pp. 10-11.
24. LaHaye, *Spirit-Controlled Temperament*, *op. cit.*, p. 8.
25. *Ibid.*, p. 110.
26. *Ibid.*, p. 7.
27. *Ibid.*, pp. 8, 45ff.
28. LaHaye, *Transformed Temperaments*, *op. cit.*, pp. 17-18.
29. *Ibid.*, p. 19.
30. *Ibid.*, pp. 30-131.
31. LaHaye, *Why You Act the Way You Do*, *op. cit.*, p. 40.
32. Florence Littauer. *Your Personality Tree*. Dallas: Word Publishing, 1986, p. 93.
33. LaHaye, *Transformed Temperaments*, *op. cit.*
34. LaHaye, *Spirit-Controlled Temperament*, *op. cit.*, p. 115.
35. LaHaye, *Transformed Temperaments*, *op. cit.*, p. 24.
36. *Ibid.*, p. 25.
37. Florence Littauer. *Personality Plus*. Fleming H. Revell Company. Tarrytown, NY: 1983, p. 15.
38. Littauer, *Your Personality Tree*, *op. cit.*, p. 18.
39. *Ibid.*, p. 34.
40. *Ibid.*
41. *Ibid.*, p. 88.

42. *Ibid.*, p. 89.
43. *Ibid.*, p. 88.
44. *Ibid.*, p. 107.
45. Florence Littauer. *Personalities in Power*. Lafayette, LA: Huntington House, 1989, pp. 221-222.
46. Littauer, *Your Personality Tree*, *op. cit.*, p. 19.
47. *Ibid.*, pp. 19-20.
48. *Ibid.*, p. 22.
49. *Ibid.*, p. 23.
50. *Ibid.*, p. 39.
51. *Ibid.*, p. 68.
52. *Ibid.*
53. *Ibid.*, pp. 71-86.
54. Littauer, *Personalities in Power*, *op. cit.*, p. 10.
55. *Ibid.*, p. 12.
56. Littauer, *Your Personality Tree*, *op. cit.*, p. 33.
57. *Ibid.*, p. 32.
58. *Ibid.*, p. 31.
59. *Ibid.*, p. 35.

Chapter 5: Personality DiSCovery?

1. Ken Voges and Ron Braund. *Understanding How Others Misunderstand You: A Unique and Proven Plan for Strengthening Personal Relationships*. Chicago: Moody Press, 1990, pp. 41-42.
2. *Ibid.*, p. 42.
3. The Personal Profile System is copyrighted by Performax Systems International, Inc., Minneapolis, 1985. Also note, that in most of their material the "i" is lower case in DiSC.
4. Voges and Braund, *op. cit.*, pp. 39-40.
5. *Ibid.*, p. 42.
6. *Ibid.*, p. 81.
7. *Ibid.*, p. 83.
8. *Ibid.*, p. 168.
9. *Ibid.*, p. 169.
10. Thomas Ice, "Personality Profiles: Help or Hindrance for Christian Living," unpublished paper.

11. Ken Voges and Ron Braund. *Understanding How Others Misunderstand You: A Unique and Proven Plan for Strengthening Personal Relationships / Workbook.* Chicago: Moody Press, 1990, p. 139.
12. Voges and Braund, *Understanding How Others Misunderstand You, op. cit.*, p. 42.
13. *Ibid.*, p. 34.
14. *Ibid.*, pp. 35-36.
15. *Ibid.*, p. 36.
16. Jay E. Adams. *The Biblical View of Self-Esteem, Self-Love, Self-Image.* Eugene, OR: Harvest House Publishers, 1986, p. 73.
17. For further information and discussion concerning self-love, refer to Martin and Deidre Bobgan, *Prophets of PsychoHeresy II*. Santa Barbara: EastGate Publishers, 1990.
18. Voges and Braund, *Understanding How Others Misunderstand You, op. cit.*, p. 27.
19. *Ibid.*, p. 36.
20. *Ibid.*, pp. 41-42.

Chapter 6: A Circus of Personality Types

1. Joel T. Johnson *et al*, "The 'Barnum Effect' Revisited: Cognitive and Motivational Factors in the Acceptance of Personality Descriptions." *Journal of Personality and Social Psychology*, Vol. 49, No. 5, 1985, p. 1378.
2. Paul Chance, "Personality's Part and Parcel." *Psychology Today*, April 1988, p. 19.
3. C. G. Jung. *Psychological Types*. Princeton, NJ: Princeton University Press, 1971, p. 516.
4. *Ibid.*, p. 518.
5. *Ibid.*, pp. 518-519.
6. *Ibid.*, p. 523.
7. Keith Harary. "The Omni-Berkeley Personality Profile," *Omni*, September 1991. p. 50.
8. David Keirsey and Marilyn Bates. *Please Understand Me: Character and Temperament Types*. Del Mar, CA: Prometheus Nemesis Books, 1978.
9. *Ibid.*, pp. 13-70.

10. Laurence Miller, "To Beat Stress, Don't Relax: Get Tough." *Psychology Today*, December 1989, pp. 62-63.
11. "Whatever happened to Type A's?" *University of California, Berkeley Wellness Letter*, Vol. 6, Issue 9, June 1990, p. 4.
12. Joann Rodgers. "Longevity Predictors: The Personality Link," *Omni Longevity*, February 1989, p. 25.
13. "Is There a Cancer Personality?" *The Johns Hopkins Medical Letter: Health After 50*, Vol. 2, Issue 1, March 1990, p. 1.
14. Robert J. Trotter. "Robert J. Sternberg: Three Heads Are Better than One." *Psychology Today*, August 1986, p. 60.
15. C. B. Lord, "I've Been Thinking. . . ." *Georgia Center Quarterly*, Vol. 3, No. 2, Winter 1988, p. 2.
16. Tony Alessandra and Jim Cathcart, "Selling Your Ideas." *Human Potential*, December 1985, pp. 28-30.
17. Lawrence L. Leshan. *Alternate Realities*. New York: Ballantine Books, 1987.
18. Jean Shinoda Bolen. *Goddesses in Everywoman: A New Psychology for Women*. San Francisco: Harper & Row, 1984.
19. "Goddesses in Our Midst." *The Terrytown Letter*, No. 46, February 1985, pp. 7-12.
20. Jean Shinoda Bolen. *Gods in Everyman*. New York: Harper & Row, 1989.
21. Robert Moore and Douglas Gillette. *King, Warrior, Magician, Lover: Rediscovering the Archetypes of the Mature Masculine*. San Francisco: Harper, 1990.
22. Pam Oslie. *Life Colors*. San Rafael, CA: New World Library, 1991.
23. "Inside the Consumer's Mind." *Newsweek*, December 1985, p. 7.
24. Gary Smalley and John Trent, "Discovering the Two Sides of Love." *Focus on the Family*, October 1990, pp. 2-5.
25. Florence Littauer. *Your Personality Tree*. Dallas: Word Publishing, 1986, p. 235.
26. David Lester, "Galen's Four Temperaments and Four-Factor Theories of Personality. *Journal of Personality Assessment*, 54 (1&2), 1990, p. 424.

27. Albert J. Bernstein and Sydney Craft Rozen. *Dinosaur Brains: Dealing with All Those Impossible People At Work*. New York: Wiley & Sons, 1989.

28. R. W. Coan, "Personality Types." *Encyclopedia of Psychology*, Vol. 3. Raymond Corsini, ed. New York: John Wiley & Sons, 1984, p. 24.

29. J. L. Andraessi, "Historical Antecedents of Somatotype theory." *Encyclopedia of Psychology*, Volume 3. Raymond Corsini, ed. New York: John Wiley & Sons, 1984, p. 353.

30. "Bloodtype reading new Japan rage; replaces astrology." *Santa Barbara News-Press*, May 16, 1984, E-5.

31. *Ibid.*

32. Littauer, *op. cit.*, p. 235.

33. John Mazziotta quoted by Kevin McKean, "Of Two Minds: Selling the Right Brain," *Discover*, 1985, p. 38.

34. Jerre Levy, "Right Brain, Left Brain: Fact and Fiction." *Psychology Today*, May 1985, p. 43.

35. Kevin McKean, "Of Two Minds: Selling the Right Brain." *Discover*, April 1985, p. 40.

36. Martin and Deidre Bobgan, *Prophets of PsychoHeresy II*. Santa Barbara: EastGate Publishers, 1990, Chapter 14.

37. "Books" (review of *The Creative Brain* by Ned Herrmann). *Training*, November 1988, p. 92.

38. "Two Brains, Four Styles." *Training*, November 1983, p. 12.

39. "Books" (review of *The Creative Brain* by Ned Herrmann), *op. cit.*, pp. 92-93.

40. "Two Brains, Four Styles," *op. cit.*, p. 12.

41. *Ibid.*, pp. 12-14.

42. Karl Albrecht, "What Color Is Your Mind?" *Professional Trainer*, Winter 1986, p. 8.

43. C. Robert Cloninger, "A Systematic Method for Clinical Description and Classification of Personality Variants." *Archives of General Psychiatry*, Vol. 44, June 1987, pp. 573-588.

44. *Ibid.*, p. 578.

45. *Ibid.*

46. Don Richard Riso. *Personality Types: Using the Enneagram for Self-Discovery*. Boston: Houghton Mifflin

Co., 1987, pp. 12-13.
47. Walter Sheer. "The Cosmology of the Fourth Way," *Gnosis*, Summer 1991, p. 27.
48. Z'ev ben Shimon Halevi. "Gurdjieff & Kabbalah: How Gurdjieff's System relates to the Tree of Life," *Gnosis*, Summer 1991, pp. 42-45.
49. Riso, *op. cit.*, p. 16.
50. Martin and Deidre Bobgan. *The Psychological Way / The Spiritual Way*. Minneapolis: Bethany House Publishers, 1979, pp. 104-108.
51. Riso, *op. cit.*, pp. 16-17.
52. *Ibid.* and Don Richard Riso. *Understanding the Enneagram: The Practical Guide to Personality Types*. Boston: Houghton Mifflin Co., 1990.
53. Riso, *Personality Types: Using the Enneagram for Self-Discovery, op. cit.*, p. 16.
54. Helen Palmer. *The Enneagram: Understanding Yourself and the Others in Your Life*. San Francisco: HarperCollins, 1991, p. *xvii*.
55. Riso, *Personality Types: Using the Enneagram for Self-Discovery, op. cit.*, p. 30.
56. Palmer, *op. cit.*, p. 38.
57. Arthur Hastings. *With the Tongues of Men and Angels*. Chicago: Holt, Rinehart and Winston, Inc., 1991, p. 95.
58. Mitchell Pacwa. "Tell Me Who I Am, O Enneagram," *Christian Research Journal*, Fall 1991, p. 19.

Chapter 7: Typology Problems

1. R. W. Coan, "Personality Types." *Encyclopedia of Psychology*, Vol. 3. Raymond Corsini, ed. New York: John Wiley & Sons, 1984, p. 23.
2. Walter Mischel. *Personality and Assessment*. New York: John Wiley & Sons, Inc., 1968, p. 146.

Chapter 8: Psychological Testing

1. Anne Anastasi. *Psychological Testing*, Sixth Edition. New York: Macmillan Publishers, 1988, p. 23.
2. *Ibid.*, p. 3.
3. *Ibid.*, p. 27.

4. *Ibid.*, p. 139.
5. *Ibid.*, p. 28.

Chapter 9: Personality Testing

1. Anne Anastasi. *Psychological Testing*, Sixth Edition. New York: Macmillan Publishers, 1988, p. 523.
2. *Ibid.*, p. 28.
3. Leslie Phillips and Joseph Smith. *Rorschach Interpretation: Advanced Technique*. New York: Grune and Stratton, 1953, p. 149.
4. Arthur Jensen. *The Sixth Mental Measurements Yearbook*. Oscar Krisen Buros, ed. Highland Park: The Gryphon Press, 1965, p. 501.
5. Charles C. McArthur. *The Seventh Mental Measurements Yearbook*. Oscar Krisen Buros, ed. Highland Park: The Gryphon Press, 1972, p. 443.
6. Jensen, *op. cit.*, p. 501.
7. Anastasi, *op. cit.*, p. 621.
8. *Ibid.*, p. 560.
9. Paul L. Houts, ed. *The Myth of Measurability*. New York: Hart Publishing Company, Inc., 1978, p. 190.
10. Martin Lasden. "The Trouble with Testing," *Training*, May 1985, p. 81.
11. Anastasi, *op. cit.*, p. 144.
12. *Ibid.*, p. 145.
13. *Ibid.*, p. 153.
14. *Ibid.*, p. 529.
15. *Ibid.*
16. Martin L. Gross. *The Brain Watchers*. New York: Random House, 1962, p. 269.
17. *Ibid.*
18. *Ibid.*, pp. 269-270.
19. *Ibid.*, p. 270.
20. *Ibid.*, p. 272.

Chapter 10: Popular Personality Tests

1. The National Research Council. *In the Mind's Eye*. Daniel Druckman and Robert A. Bjork, eds. Washington: National Academy Press, 1991, p. 96.

2. *Ibid.*, p. 99.
3. *Ibid.*, p. 101.
4. *Ibid.*
5. L. J. Cronbach and P. E. Meehl quoted by Jerry S. Wiggins, "Review of the Myers-Briggs Type Indicator." *Tenth Mental Measurements Yearbook.* Jane Close Conoley and Jack J. Kramer, eds. Lincoln: University of Nebraska Press, 1989, pp. 537-538.
6. Jerry S. Wiggins, "Review of the Myers-Briggs Type Indicator." *Tenth Mental Measurements Yearbook.* Jane Close Conoley and Jack J. Kramer, eds. Lincoln: University of Nebraska Press, 1989, p. 538.
7. Thomas Szasz. *The Myth of Psychotherapy.* Garden City: Doubleday/Anchor Press, 1978, p. 173.
8. C. G. Jung. *Memories, Dreams, Reflections.* Aniela Jaffe, ed. Richard and Clara Winston, trans. New York: Pantheon, 1963, p. 55.
9. Viktor Von Weizsaecker, "Reminiscences of Freud and Jung." *Freud and the Twentieth Century.* B. Nelson, ed. New York: Meridian, 1957, p. 72.
10. Jung, *op. cit.*, p. 183.
11. Martin and Deidre Bobgan. *PsychoHeresy: The Psychological Seduction of Christianity.* EastGate Publishers, 1987, Chapter 3.
12. David Keirsey and Marilyn Bates. *Please Understand Me: Character and Temperament Types.* Del Mar, CA: Prometheus Nemesis Books, 1978, p. 29.
13. "The Personal Profile System." Minneapolis: Performax Systems International, Inc., 1985, p. 7.
14. Sylvan J. Kaplan and Barbara E. W. Kaplan. "The Kaplan Report: A Study of the Validity of the Personal Profile System." Kaplan Associates, Chevy Chase, MD, p. 3.
15. Ellen McGinnis, "Review of the Personal Profile System." *Tenth Mental Measurements Yearbook.* Jane Close Conoley and Jack J. Kramer, eds. Lincoln: University of Nebraska Press, 1989, p. 623.
16. *Ibid.*, p. 624.
17. "Biblical Personal Profiles." Minneapolis: Performax System International, Inc., 1985, p. 20.

18. "The Personal Profile System," *op. cit.*, pp. 14-19.
19. "Biblical Personal Profiles," *op. cit.*, p. 20.
20. Christian Financial Concepts materials catalog, Gainsville, GA.
21. "Taylor-Johnson Temperament Analysis Profile," Psychological Publications, Los Angeles, 1967.
22. Robert Taylor and Lucille Morrison. *Taylor-Johnson Temperament Analysis Manual*, 1984 revision. Los Angeles: Psychological Publications, Inc., p. 23.
23. Letter on file.
24. Paul McReynolds, "Review of the Taylor-Johnson Temperament Analysis." *Tenth Mental Measurements Yearbook*. Jane Close Conoley and Jack J. Kramer, eds. Lincoln: University of Nebraska Press, 1989, p. 813.
25. H. Norman Wright, Christian Marriage Enrichment, Summer 1985 conference announcement.
26. Tim LaHaye. *Why You Act the Way You Do*. Tyndale House Publishers, Inc., 1984, p. 126.
27. American Educational Research Association, American Psychological Association, & National Council on Measurement in Education. *Standards for Educational and Psychological Testing*. Washington, DC: American Psychological Association, 1985.
28. LaHaye, *op. cit.*, pp. 365-366.
29. Gary Georgeson and Randy Fowler. "Spiritual Gift Inventory" and "Understanding Spiritual Gifts." Inter-Varsity Christian Fellowship, April 1988.
30. George Dudley, quoted by Martin Lasden in "The Trouble with Testing," *Training*, May 1985, p. 83.

Chapter 11: Why All the Deception?

1. David G. Myers. *The Inflated Self*. New York: The Seabury Press, 1980, p. 102.
2. Philippe Thiriart. "Acceptance of Personality Test Results," *Skeptical Inquirer*, Vol. 15, No. 2, Winter 1991, p. 161.
3. National Research Council. *Enhancing Human Performance: Issues, Theories, and Techniques*. Daniel Druckman and John A. Swets, eds. Washington, DC:

National Academy Press, 1988, p. 17.

4. Myers, *op. cit.*, p. 101.
5. *Ibid.*, p. 136.
6. *Ibid.*
7. *Ibid.*, p. 74.
8. *Ibid.*
9. Robert Merton. *Social Theory and Social Structure.* New York: Free Press, 1957.
10. Len Sandler. "Self-Fulfilling Prophecy: Better Management By Magic," *Training*, February 1986, p. 61.

OTHER BOOKS FROM EASTGATE

PsychoHeresy: The Psychological Seduction of Christianity by Martin and Deidre Bobgan exposes the fallacies and failures of psychological counseling theories and therapies for one purpose: to call the Church back to curing souls by means of the Word of God and the work of the Holy Spirit rather than by man-made means and opinions. Besides revealing the anti-Christian biases, internal contradictions, and documented failures of secular psychotherapy, *PsychoHeresy* examines various amalgamations of secular psychologies with Christianity and explodes firmly entrenched myths that undergird those unholy unions.

Prophets of PsychoHeresy I is a sequel to *PsychoHeresy*. It is a more detailed critique of the writings of four individuals who attempt to integrate psychological counseling theories and therapies with the Bible: Dr. Gary Collins, Dr. Lawrence Crabb, Jr., Dr. Paul Meier, and Dr. Frank Minirth. The book deals with issues, **not** personalities. For some readers, this book will be a confirmation of their suspicions. For others it will be an encouragement to be steadfast in the faith. For still others it will be a difficult challenge. Yet others will simply take a stronger stand for integration and all it implies.

Prophets of PsychoHeresy II is a critique of Dr. James C. Dobson's teachings on psychology and self-esteem. In addition, several chapters are devoted to a discussion on self-esteem from the perspective of the Bible, research, and historical development. The book evaluates teachings rather than personalities. The purpose of the book is to alert readers to the inherent spiritual dangers of psychological theories and therapies and to uphold the sufficiency of God's provisions through Jesus Christ, the Holy Spirit, and the Word of God for all matters of life and conduct.

12 Steps to Destruction: Codependency/Recovery Heresies by Martin and Deidre Bobgan provides essential information for Christians about codependency/recovery teachings, Alcoholics Anonymous, Twelve-Step groups, and addiction treatment programs. They are examined from a biblical, historical, and research perspective. The book urges believers to trust in the sufficiency of Christ and the Word of God instead of the Twelve Steps and codependency/recovery theories and therapies.

Lord of the Dance: The Beauty of the Disciplined Life by Deidre Bobgan is for women who desire a deeper, more meaningful, intimate walk with the Savior. From her background in classical ballet, Deidre draws unique parallels between the training of a ballet dancer and a disciplined, graceful walk with God.

Bethel Baptist Church
P.O. BOX 167
AUMSVILLE, OR 97325

BOOKS BY MARTIN AND DEIDRE BOBGAN

The Psychological Way/The Spiritual Way
(Bethany House Publishers)

Hypnosis and the Christian
(Bethany House Publishers)

How to Counsel from Scripture
(Moody Press)

Lord of the Dance:
The Beauty of the Disciplined Life
(EastGate Publishers)

PsychoHeresy:
The Psychological Seduction of Christianity
(EastGate Publishers)

Prophets of PsychoHeresy I
Critiquing Dr. Gary Collins, Dr. Lawrence Crabb, Jr.,
Dr. Paul Meier and Dr. Frank Minirth
(EastGate Publishers)

Prophets of PsychoHeresy II
Critiquing Dr. James Dobson
(EastGate Publishers)

12 Steps to Destruction
Codependency/Recovery Heresies
(EastGate Publishers)

For information on how to receive a free copy of
PsychoHeresy Update newsletter, please write:

EastGate Publishers
4137 Primavera Road
Santa Barbara, CA 93110